THE CRITICS DEBATE

General Editor: Michael Scott

The Critics Debate
General Editor: Michael Scott

BLAKE: SONGS OF INNOCENCE AND EXPERIENCE

David W. Lindsay

MACMILLAN

First published 1989

Published by
MACMILLAN EDUCATION LTD
Houndmills, Basingstoke, Hampshire RG21 2XS
and London
Companies and representatives
throughout the world

Printed in Hong Kong

British Library Cataloguing in Publication Data
Lindsay, David W.
Songs of innocence and experience. –
(The Critics debate).
1. Poetry in English. Blake, William, 1757–
1827. Songs of innocence & Songs of
experience – Critical studies
I. Title   II. Blake, William, *1757–1827*.
Songs of innocence & Songs of experience
821′.7
ISBN 0-333-44434-5
ISBN 0-333-44435-3 Pbk

For Cora

Contents

General Editor's Preface

Over the last few years the practice of literary criticism has become hotly debated. Methods developed earlier in the century and before have been attacked and the word 'crisis' has been drawn upon to describe the present condition of English Studies. That such a debate is taking place is a sign of the subject discipline's health. Some would hold that the situation necessitates a radical alternative approach which naturally implies a 'crisis situation'. Others would respond that to employ such terms is to precipitate or construct a false position. The debate continues but it is not the first. 'New Criticism' acquired its title because it attempted something fresh, calling into question certain practices of the past. Yet the practices it attacked were not entirely lost or negated by the new critics. One factor becomes clear: English Studies is a pluralistic discipline.

What are students coming to advanced work in English for the first time to make of all this debate and controversy? They are in danger of being overwhelmed by the cross-currents of critical approaches as they take up their study of literature. The purpose of this series is to help delineate various critical approaches to specific literary texts. Its authors are from a variety of critical schools and have approached their task in a flexible manner. Their aim is to help the reader come to terms with the variety of criticism and to introduce him or her to further reading on the subject and to a fuller evaluation of a particular text by illustrating the way it has been approached in a number of contexts. In the first part of the book a critical survey is given of some of the major ways the text has been appraised. This is done sometimes in a thematic manner, sometimes according to various 'schools' or 'approaches'. In the second part the authors provide their own appraisals of the text from their stated critical standpoint, allowing the reader the knowledge of their own particular approaches from which their views may in turn be evaluated. The series therein hopes to introduce and to elucidate criticism of authors and texts being studied and to encourage participation as the critics debate.

Michael Scott

Author's Preface

The structural principles governing this survey of Blake criticism should be clear from the table of contents; but some further explanation may be found helpful. The Introduction describes how a Blakean engraved book was created, and considers the implications of this process. The first section of Part One assesses the advantages and disadvantages of the various printed texts. The next four sections of Part One examine a range of critical approaches, with particular reference to *Songs of Innocence*. The last four sections of Part One examine a further range of critical approaches, with particular reference to *Songs of Experience*. Part Two traces the evolution of *Songs of Innocence and Experience* in the context of Blake's other writings, and gives closer attention to eight poems. The list of references identifies the critical works mentioned, and offers suggestions for further reading.

Alan Bellringer, Tony Brown, Tom Corns, John Eadie, Peter Field, Ian Gregson, Chris Jones, Margaret Locherbie-Cameron, Brian Mastin, Mark Sinfield and Bill Tydeman have assisted me in a variety of ways. I am also grateful to Pat Pritchard and Joyce Williams, who typed the manuscript, and to the library staff of the University College of North Wales. My greatest debt, as always, is to my wife.

Bangor 1988 *David W. Lindsay*

Introduction

Works of literature assume many forms, in consequence of the various modes of literary production which are promoted by technical and socioeconomic conditions. The form in which we encounter a work may be very different from the form in which it was created, and critical analysis must take account of the original form and of the historical context implicit in it. A proper understanding of the Child ballads becomes possible only if we take account of the musical and narrative techniques which are encouraged by oral transmission. A play written for performance in the Globe Theatre has to be interpreted in the light of what we know about acting and stagecraft in Shakespeare's London. A monthly-part novel by Dickens should be read with some appreciation of the artistic techniques associated with monthly publication. In these cases and in many others, the reader of a modern printed text has to be aware that this form is entirely different from that in which the work was created. The first step towards intelligent understanding is to envisage the work in its original form, which in most cases can be seen as the form in which it was most truly itself.

The work that we know as *Songs of Innocence and Experience* was in its earliest complete form a Blakean engraved book, and in seeking to interpret it we must recognise the artistic consequences of the unusual manner in which such a book was produced and distributed. Although Blake is now internationally celebrated as a writer and an artist, he was little known in those capacities during his lifetime. He was trained as an engraver, and for most of his life he earned a rather modest living by engraving illustrations for the published texts of other people's writings. None of his important literary works was printed and published in the then customary fashion, and some of them remained in manuscript until long after his death. Many of them were produced and distributed by the author himself, with the aid of a process which he devised about 1788 and continued to use until 1822. That process, which is described in detail by Essick (1980, 85–120), was in modern terminology a form of relief etching; but Blake himself called it engraving, and the ordinary reader of his poetry can safely ignore the technical distinction. What matters is that Blake etched or engraved the texts of these books himself on copperplate, enriching them as he did so by adding decorative and illustrative designs. Every copy of a Blakean engraved book had to be handprinted page by page, and most copies were then coloured either by the author or by his wife Catherine. The completed books were sold individually by the author; but they were scarcely advertised, and the sales were very small.

These facts about the production and distribution of Blake's engraved books have large consequences for his method of composition, and for the way in which the texts of his engraved books should be read. Although the manuscript evidence suggests that composition of the text commonly preceded invention of the design, it is clear that by the engraving stage text and design had often become so intricately related that neither could be fully interpreted without reference to the other. There are many plates in which the design significantly modifies the meaning of the text, and some in which the text is so enigmatic as to be almost incomprehensible without the clarification offered by the design. There are instances, too, in which the text and the design comment ironically on one another, so that the full import of the plate is altogether more complex than the apparent sense of either component on its own. And in any case it is scarcely possible to draw a clear distinction between text and design. Variations in the size and character of Blake's engraved script contribute to the visual artistry and atmosphere of each plate; and the seemingly decorative images of animal and vegetable life often function as unorthodox punctuation-marks, as marks of division within the text, or as indicators of pace and mood like the words on a musical score. A modern printed text cannot adequately represent a Blakean engraved book; and the most important aid to understanding is therefore a reproduction of the book as Blake produced it. Anyone who wishes to achieve a full appreciation of *Songs of Innocence and Experience* should acquire a copy of the reproduction of that work published in 1970 by Oxford University Press. This has a short introduction and a simple commentary by Sir Geoffrey Keynes; but its main value lies in its fifty-four colour-plates, which allow us to see the poems as Blake wanted his readers to see them. Serious criticism of these poems cannot begin until they have been studied in the context of Blake's engraved designs.

Even a perfect reproduction, however, can represent only one copy of a Blakean engraved book; and one of the consequences of Blake's unusual method of production is that different copies may differ so radically that one might almost regard each of them as an independent work. The natural sequence of composition for an individual plate would begin with the drafting and revising of a text, proceed through the designing of an illustration and the engraving of a copperplate to the printing of a page, and end with the colouring of that page by hand. These stages in the process of composition might follow closely upon one another, but they might in other cases take place over a long period; and the processes of printing and colouring could be repeated, perhaps after a long interval, to produce a new copy. This does not mean, however, that these stages necessarily followed one another in this simple pattern during the composition of a whole engraved book. Because Blake was his own printer and his own publisher, he could begin engraving the plates for a book before he had finished writing the text. He could, after engraving some of the plates, make large alterations or additions to the still unengraved portion of a partly engraved work. When some or all of the plates had been engraved, he could change his mind about the order in which they were to be printed. Even after some copies of a work had been printed, coloured and sold, Blake could refashion it by introducing new plates and rearranging existing ones, so that later copies assumed a different form and conveyed a different message. And he could take plates which had been engraved for one book and reuse them in another book with a new title page. Alterations to individual copperplates were more problematic, because they tended to spoil the harmony of the designs, but it was possible to delete words which had become inappropriate because of changes elsewhere in the book. And if a printed page was being coloured, the colouring could be used to obliterate unwanted parts of the printed text or to alter the meaning of the engraved design. The choice of different colour-schemes for different copies could produce startlingly different visual effects, and with some plates could make the same engraved shape suggest vegetation in one version and fire in another.

In seeking to interpret a Blakean engraved book, therefore, we have to take account of the special freedoms and constraints associated with Blake's distinctive method of production; and we have to remember that different copies of the book may have been produced at different stages in Blake's life, and may differ quite fundamentally from one another.

Songs of Innocence and Experience, in particular, is not a single composition whose publication can be assigned to a specific year. It is a work which underwent many large mutations over a long period of time, and whose successive forms are related to different stages in Blake's personal, ideological and artistic development. The title page for *Songs of Innocence* bears the date 1789, but this tells us merely that Blake engraved this title page in that year. Some of the poems which he then included in *Songs of Innocence* had been drafted much earlier, and had initially appeared in quite different contexts. Other poems, almost certainly composed after the engraving of the title page, had become part of *Songs of Innocence* by the time Blake completed a book with that title. Around 1788–90 *Songs of Innocence* emerged as a complete and self-sufficient work which, like other Blakean engraved books, took rather different forms in different copies. The concept of Innocence as a prelapsarian state of total harmony implied the existence of a fallen state whose divisions and conflicts made it unlike Innocence. The creation of a collection of poems about Innocence did not, however, imply the subsequent creation of a complementary collection of poems about that fallen state. Blake was prompted to compose such a complementary collection by the changes in his worldview which took place in the early 1790s; and it was not until 1794 that he engraved a title page for *Songs of Experience* and a general title page inscribed *Songs of Innocence and of Experience Showing the Two Contrary States of the Human Soul*. In creating this new engraved book in two parts, he used both the copperplates designed for *Songs of Innocence* and new copperplates which he engraved around 1793–5. The new scheme involved some rearrangement and reinterpretation of existing material, and four poems which had been included in some copies of *Songs of Innocence* were now transposed into the second half of the two-part sequence. That sequence continued to change, however, with significant modifications both in the order of the plates and in the typical colour-scheme, as new copies were produced over a period of years. The last addition to the text, the lyric entitled 'To Tirzah', was composed and engraved many years after the other poems in the book; but it became a part of the quasi-definitive order which was established by the copies of *Songs of Innocence and Experience* that Blake printed and coloured with his wife's help in his later life. The text of these late copies may reasonably be accepted as the authoritative form of the book; but interpretation of the book, and of individual poems within it, must take cognisance of the long and complex process by which this authoritative form was achieved. The reader has to attend both to the book's evolution and to its artistic shape at every stage in that evolution.

Part One: Survey

Defining the text

Over the last hundred years a large number of distinguished scholars have directed their energies to the editing of Blake's literary work. The task they have undertaken has been an impossible one, since no printed text can adequately represent either a Blakean engraved book or a much-altered manuscript like that of *The Four Zoas*. Yet the impossible undertaking has also been necessary and valuable, because Blake's writings present innumerable problems of the sort that are commonly addressed rather by editors than by critics. The first attempt to produce a complete edition of Blake's work, that of E.J. Ellis and W.B. Yeats, was grossly inaccurate and is now more significant for students of Yeats than for students of Blake. The edition which established a generally reliable text was that of Sir Geoffrey Keynes, which appeared in three volumes in 1925. Keynes's work has in some respects been superseded by that of later scholars, but in its time it was a historic achievement comparable with Grierson's edition of Donne. In the context of this undertaking *Songs of Innocence and Experience* was a relatively unproblematic text; but a comparison of Keynes's later one-volume editions of Blake's writings reveals some of the special problems which an editor of that text has to face.

In the Centenary Edition published by the Nonesuch Press in 1927, Keynes presented Blake's writings not in a single chronological sequence but under such generic headings as 'Didactic and Symbolic Works' and 'Marginalia'. Within this framework the poems composing *Songs of Innocence and Experience* formed a group on their own; and Keynes explained that he had printed them in the order which Blake adopted 'in the majority of the later copies of the book'. This arrangement has obvious advantages for students of *Songs of Innocence and Experience*, since it gives us the text of that book in the sequence Blake finally chose, and allows us to appreciate the significant juxtapositions which the author devised. On the other hand, the separation of Blake's lyrical poetry from his prophetic and mythical poetry creates a misleading impression, since these elements in his work actually developed side by side all through his career. In the edition published by the Nonesuch Press in 1957 and reissued in the Oxford Standard Authors series in 1966, Keynes reverted to the strictly chronological arrangement which he had followed in his 1925 volumes. This policy places the text of *Songs of Innocence*, as engraved around 1789, between texts of two mythical narratives from the same period, *Tiriel* and *The Book of Thel*; and it links the poems engraved around 1794 for *Songs of Experience* to books roughly contemporary with them, such as the prophetic poem entitled *America* and the pseudo-biblical poem ultimately called *The Book of Urizen*. This arrangement highlights the initial self-sufficiency of *Songs of Innocence*, and draws attention to the thematic links between Blake's lyrical and non-lyrical poems; but it achieves these advantages by sacrificing the artistic unity of the poet's most celebrated book, which in its final form was much more than the sum of its parts. Since the benefits of these two editorial procedures cannot be combined, it is clear that no single edition can offer a wholly satisfactory text of *Songs of Innocence and Experience* in the context of Blake's literary development. A reader who has taken Keynes's reproduction of *Songs of Innocence and Experience* as his primary text, however, may usefully study it in conjunction with Keynes's Oxford Standard Authors edition of 1966. The evidence provided by that edition enables one to supplement a coherent response to *Songs of Innocence and Experience* as a book with appropriate comparisons between the poems in that book and the other Blakean writings contemporary with them.

In comparing the reproduction with either of Keynes's one-volume editions, however, one encounters another textual problem scarcely less perplexing than that of sequence. Blake's engraved books, like his manuscripts, are sparsely and sometimes ambiguously punctuated; and a responsible editor naturally tries to assist his readers by supplying punctuation which will both clarify the syntax and identify phrases in direct speech. In supplying that punctuation, however, the editor has to commit the reader to particular interpretations; and such commitment may sometimes impede understanding, either because the editor has adopted the wrong interpretation or because the ambiguity created by lack of punctuation was a significant factor in the text's rhetorical strategy. For many of the poems in *Songs of Innocence and Experience* Keynes chooses to supply quotation-marks in order to distinguish the different voices which are audible in the text; but these quotation-marks are often intrusive and sometimes damaging. One of Blake's characteristic devices in *Songs of Innocence* is the presentation of a monologue which subsumes a dialogue: the implication is that the primary speaker has achieved complete empathy with the secondary speaker and is thus in a position to undertake both roles. This technique can be seen in the dialogue between child and lamb in 'Spring', which Keynes wisely leaves without quotation-marks; and it can be seen again in the dialogue between mother and child in 'Infant Joy', where the editorial quotation-marks contradict Blake's meaning by insisting on distinction instead of unity. The absence of quotation-marks is a significant feature of Blake's engraved text in both these poems; and it is equally significant in the first 'Nurse's Song', in 'The Little Black Boy', and in the 'Introduction' to *Songs of Experience*. It is closely related to that merging of identities which we recognise, especially in 'The Lamb' and 'A Cradle Song', as a manifestation both of Innocence and of redemptive love.

There have been great advances in Blake scholarship since Keynes's edition of 1925, and many editors have contributed to the establishment of more complete and more accurate texts. These developments have been less significant for *Songs of Innocence and Experience* than for Blake's longer poems, but relevant material of some importance can be found in several major publications. The earliest and most influential of these is David V. Erdman's edition of Blake's poetry and prose, which was issued by Doubleday and Company in 1965. Affected by the systematic interpretation of Blake's work which Northrop Frye had expounded in *Fearful Symmetry*, Erdman in this volume identified the engraved books or 'Works in Illuminated Printing' as the 'major canon' of Blake's writings. He placed the texts of these canonical works in the forefront of his edition, relegating works preserved in other modes to subordinate positions; and he printed each of the engraved books in its latest and most authoritative form. Although he placed *Songs of Innocence and Experience* immediately after *The Book of Thel*, his text followed the usual arrangement of the late copies; and he reproduced Blake's minimal punctuation, with no question-marks in 'The Lamb' and no quotation-marks anywhere. His textual notes on *Songs of Innocence and Experience* gave a full account of textual variants for the twenty-two poems which survive in manuscript versions. Erdman's edition included an interpretative commentary by Harold Bloom; but this commentary ignored *Songs of Innocence and Experience*, choosing rather to elucidate the more obvious difficulties of Blake's mythical narratives.

The Doubleday edition was followed in 1971 by an edition in the Longman Annotated Poets series. Although Erdman was again responsible for the text, he worked within the rules laid down by F.W. Bateson as general editor; and this meant that the poems were presented in chronological order and in modernised spelling and punctuation. In these respects the Longman edition resembled Keynes's Oxford Standard Authors edition; but it fell short of that work in omitting the prose, and surpassed it in offering a detailed commentary. This commentary, which was the work of W.H. Stevenson, avoided bold generalities of the sort favoured by Bloom; but it enlisted the traditional resources of literary scholarship to identify and resolve many local obscurities in Blake's text.

In 1973 Erdman published a facsimile edition of Blake's notebook, the manuscript volume whose contents include drafts of eighteen poems later included in *Songs of Experience*. This admirably scholarly edition is illuminating not only because it shows Blake's developing conception of such poems as 'The Tyger' but also because it allows us to compare drafts of those poems with other material scribbled or sketched on the same pages. In 1975 Erdman produced a volume entitled *The Illuminated Blake*, which included black-and-white reproductions of all Blake's engraved books. Erdman's detailed interpretations of the designs are sometimes over-ingenious, but his commentary offers much useful evidence about the plate sequence and colouring of the various copies. For students of the songs, *The Illuminated Blake* is more immediately helpful than the two-volume edition of Blake's *Writings* edited by G.E. Bentley Jr and published in 1978 by the Clarendon Press. There is a wealth of factual information, however, in Bentley's meticulous bibliographical notes; and those notes, unexciting as they may appear, should help to give substance and precision to future explorations of Blake's imaginative development.

Antecedents of Innocence

As we have seen, *Songs of Innocence and Experience* grew out of *Songs of Innocence*, which around 1790 was a complete and self-sufficient work. Any investigation into the origins of the larger and later work, therefore, has to begin by considering the origins of the shorter and earlier one. The origins of *Songs of Innocence* have been much discussed by scholars and critics, the discussion taking three principal forms. First, there have been attempts to interpret the various anticipations of *Songs of Innocence* in Blake's earlier writings, and in particular to determine the significance of five manuscript lyrics which were later adapted and engraved for *Songs of Innocence*. Second, there have been critical interpretations of *Songs of Innocence* and of individual poems therein as contributions to the European tradition of pastoral literature and more specifically of pastoral lyric. Third, there have been examinations of the book as a contribution to the eighteenth-century tradition of religious and didactic writing for children, especially as that tradition combined text and illustration and drew on the methods of English hymnody.

There are significant anticipations of *Songs of Innocence* in *Poetical Sketches*, the collection of Blake's juvenilia which was printed in 1783. They include a number of neo-Elizabethan songs, the best of which is the 'Mad Song' inspired by the six 'Mad Songs' collected in Percy's *Reliques of Ancient English Poetry* (1765). No less significant is the verse-tale about children at play entitled 'Blind-Man's Buff', which echoes the winter song in *Love's Labour's Lost* and relates the children's mishaps to society's lapse from a primeval harmony. Shakespeare's winter song is echoed again in one of the three pastoral lyrics which were transcribed into a copy of *Poetical Sketches* about 1783–4 and first printed by Keynes in 1910. These lyrics are attributed to 'a shepherd', 'a young shepherd' and 'an old shepherd', and the first and third of them use the word 'Innocence' in the context of a moral and subjective pastoralism like that of Amiens' songs in *As You Like It*. An altered text of the second poem was engraved for *Songs of Innocence* with the title 'Laughing Song', and critics have compared the two versions in order to define the developing quality of Blake's pastoralism. Keynes (1970, 137) reminds us that the young Blake composed tunes for his own poems, and suggests that the 'sweet chorus' of 'Laughing Song' requires 'a simple merry tune'. Hirsch (1964, 188–90) notes that the engraved version is 'made more vigorous' by the reordering of the stanzas, but concludes that the changes are 'not substantial' and that the poem 'belongs to the end of Blake's literary apprenticeship'. Gardner (1986, 50–52) observes that the replacement of 'Edessa, and Lyca, and Emilie' with 'Mary and Susan and Emily' moves the poem into 'familiar country', but argues that the unchanged epithet 'painted' is inappropriate to English songbirds.

More perplexing anticipations of *Songs of Innocence* appear in the fragment of prose fiction commonly known as *An Island in the Moon*, which Blake composed about 1784. Proceeding in the manner of Sterne's *Tristram Shandy* from satire on learned folly to celebration of natural impulse, this work reaches its climax and turning-point in the comic explosion of Chapter 10. Chapter 11 describes a 'merry meeting at the house of Steelyard the Lawgiver', and the songs which the characters sing on this occasion include early versions of the poems engraved for *Songs of Innocence* as 'Holy Thursday', 'Nurse's Song' and 'The Little Boy Lost'. The fact that these poems are here sung by characters named Obtuse Angle, Mrs Nannicantipot and Quid the Cynic has occasioned much critical debate. According to Frye (1947, 192), their appearance in this satirical context shows that 'the idea of associating them with parallel songs of experience was already in Blake's mind'. After exploring their social and literary background, Erdman (1954, 107–16) agreed that they were 'at least ironic' in their original context, but argued that they were 'plainly not presented as satire' in *Songs of Innocence*. Hirsch (1964, 17) decisively rejected Frye's view, contending that the characters' responses to Obtuse Angle's song showed it to be 'more an agent than an object of satire'.

So far as 'Holy Thursday' and 'Nurse's Song' are concerned, one can agree with Gardner (1986, 23) that their 'arrival . . . in a satirical setting . . . has caused much more trouble than it need have done'. When Quid's song was engraved as 'The Little Boy Lost', however, its atmosphere was changed by the removal of 'the anapests and the mockery' (Erdman, 1965, 714); and its meaning was transformed by the addition of a sequel entitled 'The Little Boy Found'. The cynic's comprehensive denial of all ideals was thus transmuted into the first half of a two-part parable about Innocence endangered and re-established. That Blake's transformation of his earlier vision was not entirely successful is suggested by the response of Larrissy (1985, 28 and 61). Associating 'The Little Boy Found' with other 'innocent imaginings' which show a 'severely limited' understanding of the world, Larrissy sees this 'comforting end to a disturbing story' as answering 'a need for security which is . . . potentially debilitating and enslaving'.

Anticipations of *Songs of Innocence* in Blake's earlier writings highlight the book's dramatic and linguistic subtlety, but its imaginative scope emerges more clearly from a consideration of its pastoralism. Pastoral is an urban mode of Alexandrian origin, which achieves its effects by imaging a rural world notably different from that inhabited by author and readers. Its implications are at once idealistic and satirical, and despite its classical origins it lends itself to Christian reinterpretation. Medieval artists associated the Golden Age with the Garden of Eden, and used pastoral devices to honour Christ as the Good Shepherd. In Reformation literature the shepherd and his flock are often emblematic of the clergyman and his congregation. Christian humanist ideals found expression, in Renaissance Italy and Elizabethan England, through important sub-genres like the pastoral romance, the pastoral drama and the pastoral lyric. Two of Blake's juvenile poems echo the attenuated pastoralism of the young Alexander Pope, but the pastoralism of *Songs of Innocence* is Elizabethan rather than Augustan. Blake's songs follow those of Shakespeare in celebrating not an idyllic landscape but an integrated humanity, and the pastoral technique of implied comparison thus makes the book an imaginative interpretation of the Fall of Man. In transposing the argument of *Paradise Lost* from classical epic to pastoral lyric, Blake voices that celebration and critique of Milton which is a recurrent feature of his literary and artistic work.

Dike (1961, 375) finds in *Songs of Innocence* a 'convincing reminder that pastoral, as a way of relating the human realities, can be toughly honest'. In his discussions of 'The Shepherd' (1964, 28–30 and 174–5), Hirsch stressed the 'radically immanental Christianity' of *Songs of Innocence*, arguing that this poem defines 'a religious perspective in which man and God are not simply analogous but essentially one'. By fusing 'the Old Testament symbol of the Shepherd with the New Testament symbol of the Lamb', Blake here communicates the sense of trust and mutual responsiveness which is promoted by the divine presence in every feature of its pastoral world. In his discussions of 'The

Ecchoing Green' (1964, 39–41 and 176–7), Hirsch claims that this text 'traces the entire cycle of human life' within a poetic landscape which fuses 'the natural with the prophetic'. Comparing 'The Ecchoing Green' with a song about village sports in *Poetical Sketches*, he concludes that 'Blake managed to deepen his unpromising early use of the pastoral mode only by bringing it to the service of a religious vision'. Gardner (1986, 15–21 and 46–50) relates Blake's pastoralism to the fosterhomes provided around Wimbledon Common for pauper children from his district of London. Insisting that the lamb is central to the poet's pastoral thinking, Gardner points out that the lamb is 'a symbol of caring'. He argues that both text and illustrations of 'The Ecchoing Green' relate 'maternal cherishing and family care' to 'participation in a community', and that the 'chief motivation' in the poem is not 'instinctive joy' but rather 'human need'. He is less interested in the religious dimension of Blake's pastoralism than in the background of personal involvement which enabled the poet to transform 'commonplace pastoral stuff' into the 'strange and inimitable complex of ideas' that we encounter in 'Spring'.

While *Songs of Innocence* is deeply indebted to the pastoral tradition in its thematic structure, its outward form is that of a collection of religious lyrics for children. Earlier books of that type included John Bunyan's *A Book for Boys and Girls* (1686), Isaac Watts's *Divine Songs Attempted in Easy Language for the Use of Children* (1715), Charles Wesley's *Hymns for Children* (1763), and Christopher Smart's *Hymns for the Amusement of Children* (1770). Such works sought to counteract the pernicious influence of popular chapbooks, and Blake was familiar with the genre because the publisher Joseph Johnson had employed him to engrave illustrations for Anna Letitia Barbauld's *Hymns in Prose for Children* (1781). Blake's relationship to this convention was noted as early as 1806, when a contributor to the *Monthly Review* declared him 'certainly very inferior to Dr. Watts', and it has been amply documented by scholars of the last fifty years. Pinto (1944, 214–23) notes the importance of animal, bird, insect and flower poems, and shows how Blake in 'A Cradle Song' transposes Watts's 'A Cradle Hymn' into 'a new poetic idiom'. Raine (1969, I, 30–33) claims that Watts's chief contribution to *Songs of Innocence* was that he 'represented all that to Blake seemed most wrong with the religious morality of the time in its special relation to childhood'.

Holloway (1968, 30–54) argues that Blake was both imitating and criticising his predecessors in this mode, and that such poems as 'The Divine Image' and 'On Another's Sorrow' employ the versification of eighteenth-century hymnody to undermine its typical values. Shrimpton (1976) compares Blake's poems with hymns by Wesley and others, arguing that *Songs of Innocence* presents 'the best possible defences and interpretations of the act of protection in its familial, religious, and political contexts'. Glen (1983, 8–32) develops Holloway's suggestion that Blake was engaged in a 'debate' with writers like Watts and Barbauld, and suggests that in this debate he was 'foregrounding and exploring the problematic nature of that process whereby men seek to categorise and label experience'. These studies, while less speculative than most explorations of Blake's pastoralism, serve a similar purpose in clarifying his imaginative critique of eighteenth-century culture.

Reading the designs

Most interpreters of *Songs of Innocence and Experience* have paid at least lip-service to the principle that text and designs in a Blakean engraved book should be regarded as aspects of a single artistic statement. Some discussions, however, have laid particular emphasis on the designs, assessing their quality as works of art and examining the various ways in which they enrich and modify the literary impact of the poems. Critics whose commitment is rather to art history than to literary history have examined the formal properties of Blake's compositions, relating them to those of artists whose work he knew from engravings. In this area, as in that of literary analysis, scholars have sought to identify the antecedents of Blake's method and to trace its development within his work. In many instances interpretations founded on the designs have been greatly influenced by the expectations of critics with a particular interest in Blake's views on social injustice, on sexuality, or on religion. Some commentators have found inspiration in the designs for boldly original interpretations of enigmatic lyrics, and such interpretations have become the basis for long-running critical disputes. On the other hand, a scrupulous wariness of imposing non-Blakean meanings on the designs has led other commentators into a plate-by-plate analysis which gives close attention to the most minute and apparently insignificant details. All these approaches have their distinctive advantages and their characteristic dangers.

The process by which the engraved books were produced is described by Todd (1971, 20–23), and more expansively discussed by Essick (1980, 83–164). Blunt (1959, 44–63) considers the artistic consequences of this process, comparing the 'more conventional' plates with the illustrations of Blake's associate Thomas Stothard. He finds 'a perfect fusion of text and decoration' in the plates for 'The Divine Image', 'The Blossom' and 'Infant Joy', and claims that in those plates at least Blake has created 'a type of illuminated page for which no parallel can be found except in the finest manuscripts of the Middle Ages'. Raine (1970, 41–62) associates the 'energy and spontaneity' of Blake's designs for *Songs of Innocence* with his 'realization that life . . . is not subject to the forces of nature' and that consciousness 'moves freely where it wills'. Bass (in Erdman and Grant 1970, 196–213) analyses the impact of vertical, horizontal and diagonal movements in the designs, and gives extensive consideration to such motifs as the 'great reversed "S" curve' in the design for 'The Divine Image'. Bindman (1977, 58–65) considers the designs in the context of Blake's development as an artist, giving particular attention to the visual connections between *Songs of Innocence* and other eighteenth-century books in which the texts are surrounded by decorative borders.

Lister (1968, 19) sees a clue to 'the origin of Blake's illuminated books' in a fragmentary dialogue towards the end of *An Island in the Moon*, which suggests that the original plan was not to unite text and design in each plate but rather to alternate pages of text with full-page illustrations. Further evidence of this plan is offered in *Songs of Innocence* by the 'Introduction' and the frontispiece, which all interpreters see as being closely connected. Blunt (1959, 45 and Plate 16) compares the symmetrical ovals flanking the 'Introduction' with medieval representations of the Tree of Jesse, and several critics have discussed Blake's possible debt to illuminated manuscripts. Lister (1968, 19–20) finds a possible connection in the engraved devotional books produced by early printers; and Hagstrum (1964, 31) demonstrates that Blake could in 1786 have seen a fifteenth-century Book of Hours at the shop of James Edwards, who later commissioned his illustrations to *Night Thoughts*. Erdman (1975, 45–6) gives a meticulous description of the eight designs enclosed in Blake's Tree of Jesse, but makes no attempt to interpret them as a sequence. Leader (1981, 73) concludes that they are 'too small or too indistinctly printed and colored to be identified with much certainty', and that they merely 'suggest a range of moods and human activities'.

The text of the 'Introduction' offers the pastoral lyricist's account of the composition of his songs, identifying the laughing child as their inspiration and the lamb as their appropriate subject; and this programmatic statement about *Songs of Innocence* finds its visual equivalent in a full-page illustration, where the piper looks up to the cloud-borne child while his sheep graze securely between intertwining trees. The shift to combining text and design on the same plate, however, led Blake to use his full-page illustration to the 'Introduction' as a frontispiece for *Songs of Innocence*, and the later decision to produce a two-part sequence led him to engrave a complementary frontispiece for *Songs of Experience*. Keynes (1970, 131) describes the frontispiece to *Songs of Innocence* as a 'literal illustration' to the 'Introduction', but adds that the 'twining trunks of the tree on the poet's left' introduce 'a symbol not mentioned in the poem'. Leader (1981, 61–4) rejects Keynes's suggestion that this symbol represents 'earthly love', and argues that the frontispiece establishes the 'enclosed setting' as a 'key visual motif' associated with the 'secure, unthreatened' state which the whole book celebrates. Mitchell (1978, 4–9) discusses the frontispiece to *Songs of Innocence* in connection with that to *Songs of Experience*, suggesting that the process by which we interpret their contrasting visual statements 'entails a good deal more than simple matching or translating of visual signs into verbal'.

Much controversy has been generated by those lyrics in which Blake allows innocent speakers to articulate their responses to a fallen society, and interpreters of such poems have often invoked the authority of Blake's designs in support of their readings. Keynes (1970, 139) says that the text of 'Holy Thursday' is 'probably . . . ironic', and that the irony is 'driven home by the regimented and uniformed processions of children depicted at the top and bottom of the plate'. Gardner (1986, 36–7) argues that this image of a 'lively procession' conveys a 'sense of relaxed formality and assurance . . . without a trace of regimentation'. Hirsch (1964, 184–6) claims that the 'affirmation of visionary joy' in 'The Chimney Sweeper' is 'more triumphant than in any other poem of the series', and finds confirmation of this in a design which shows children 'leaping and laughing in the sun'. Leader (1981, 46–7), noting that Blake had to 'squeeze' this design into 'a half-inch strip along the bottom of the plate', argues that since 'the great block of text presses down upon Tom's dream like a weight' the poem is in fact illuminated by the design's 'cramped and unpleasant appearance'. Comparable disagreements have arisen over the two illustrations to 'The Little Black Boy', which represent the speaker's memory of his mother's loving instruction and his vision of himself presenting the white child to Christ. Keynes (1970, 134–5) says that the mother in the first plate is 'looking towards the rising sun', though her gaze is in reality fixed on her child. Hirsch (1964, 181) claims that the sun 'symbolizes the beginning of the little boy's earthly life', and Raine (1969, I, 10–13) associates it with ' "eternity's sun rise", in which the angels always dwell'; but neither considers the significance of the child's raised arm, which points towards a different sun. In the second plate Hirsch sees the children 'in Eternity with their heavenly parent', and Keynes finds evidence in 'the water and the vegetation' that 'heaven may be found on earth'. In a long discussion, Leader (1981, 108–17) argues that 'the picture the black boy's mother paints of Heaven' is here shown to be 'an illusion', and that the seated figure is 'the Christ not of Innocence but . . . of institutionalized religion'.

Interpretation of the designs becomes more important and still more controversial when the reader needs their assistance even to identify a poem's subject. The obvious examples in *Songs of Innocence* are 'The Blossom', 'Infant Joy' and 'Spring', whose texts are in isolation so cryptic as to seem almost meaningless. In the earliest major commentary on *Songs of Innocence and Experience*, Wicksteed (1928, 122–9) interprets 'The Blossom' as a female monologue expressing the innocent sensibility's apprehension of sexual union, and 'Infant Joy' as a lyric for three voices in which the moment of conception is celebrated by father, mother and child. Wicksteed sees the design for 'The Blossom' as 'a poetic and symbolic rendering of the phallus prone and erect, a pillar of vegetable flame breaking at the crest into multitudinous life'; and he notes that one of the 'many happy spirits' represented has 'found its home' with the winged female above the title. He finds a complementary image of conception in the 'opening flower with its attendant bud' which dominates the design for 'Infant Joy';

and he describes the group within this flower as 'an Annunciation scene' in which the 'divine messenger' represents 'the life-factor of the father'. These interpretations, though endorsed by Keynes (1970, 135 and 140–44), have been treated sceptically by later interpreters (Stevenson 1971, 64–5; Gardner 1986, 52–6); but they remain more coherent and more plausible than any that have been offered in their place. Hirsch, who declares flatly that he 'cannot accept' Wicksteed's explication of 'The Blossom', is himself responsible for an equally bold and illuminating reading of the designs for 'Spring' (1964, 38–9 and 198–9). Seeing the movement from the first illustration to the second as one 'from actual life to Eternity', Hirsch interprets the command 'Sound the Flute!' as 'a pastoral prophecy of the last trumpet' and perceives 'a weight of apocalyptic meaning' in the words 'Little Lamb/Here I am'. This reading of 'Spring' as a pastoral reinterpretation of the Last Judgement has caused understandable embarrassment, but its validity is confirmed by such details as the four angels in Blake's marginal decorations.

Erdman's commentaries on the designs (1975, 41–96) offer no such breathtaking revelations, but much can be learned from his meticulous description of the details visible on a range of copies. His comments on the first plate of 'Night', for example, invite us to see in this nocturnal scene not only the vine-encircled tree arising from the sleeping lion's waterside cave but also minute images of the moon and the descending sun, of seven stars and seven angels, of two doves, and of a 'robed figure' who is contemplating 'the peaceful night as a heavenly garden'. Although he is sometimes unhelpful with obviously problematic images like the five human figures in the second plate of 'Night', Erdman usefully insists on giving close attention to everything that Blake included in his designs.

Voices of Innocence

As we have seen, four poems which Blake engraved for *Songs of Innocence* had appeared earlier in contexts which identified them as the songs of a young shepherd, Obtuse Angle, Mrs Nannicantipot's mother, and Quid the Cynic. Many of the other poems in *Songs of Innocence*, such as 'A Cradle Song' and 'The Little Black Boy', are dramatic lyrics for clearly-identified speakers.

Even the poems whose speakers are less sharply distinguished from the poet, such as 'Night' and 'The Divine Image', are marked as dramatic lyrics by their appearance in a volume which gives definition and expression to the state of Innocence. Innocence may be provisionally described as a state in which the human faculties are perfectly integrated, in which no being can refuse full sympathy to another, and in which the harmony of Man, God and Nature is too complete to allow a non-human conception of divinity or matter. The separate poems contribute to Blake's celebration of this ideal, and draw added significance from it; and many critics have sought to interpret them by analysing the intricacies of their psychological drama. This can require some investigation of relevant social and intellectual contexts, such as the charity-school controversy or the writings of Swedenborg. It also involves considering how the speakers of individual lyrics relate to the author and readership implied by the whole book, and how the speaker of each poem interacts with the other characters whom that poem invokes. With the greatest poems, such as 'The Chimney Sweeper', it can be a complex adventure merely to participate in the speaker's changing awareness from the first line through to the last.

That these poems use the dramatic-lyric form to communicate a distinctive mode of vision is especially obvious in 'A Dream'. Relating this poem to oral tradition, Adlard (1972, 48–9) points out that the dor-beetle is known as 'the watchman' because it flies after sunset with a loud humming noise, and that a folksong known to Blake asserts that the glow-worm 'lights us home to bed' when there is no moonlight. Comparing 'A Dream' with lyrics about insects by Bunyan and Watts, Pinto (1957, 76–8) argues that the speaker, instead of taking the ant as a subject for allegorical or generalised moralising, attempts to 'enter with imaginative sympathy into the child-world of smallness, helplessness and bewilderment'. Hirsch (1964, 203–4) claims that there is 'a touch of humor in the poet's sympathy with the insects', but sees the predominant tone as one of 'unqualified trust in God's beneficence', and describes the dreamer's world as 'one in which everyone is both guarded and guardian'. After tracing 'the impulse of mutual solicitude' through the various characters of the insect drama, Gillham (1966, 206–9) argues that we are 'meant to see the speaker as a child', and that the child's dream expresses 'the knowledge of mutual care as a force active in the world'. Glen

(1983, 184–5) draws attention to the 'ready empathy' which makes the word 'heart-broke' as relevant to the dreamer as to the ant, and shows how such empathy creates a world of 'unselfregarding' impulses in which there is 'no separation of self from other'. The reader of 'A Dream' is invited to share that creative intuition of ungrudging responsiveness through which the speaker's sense of angelic protection has been confirmed.

The speaker of 'The Lamb' is clearly identified as a child both in the illustration and in the text, and the identification is confirmed by the poem's rhythms and thought-processes. Hirsch (1964, 177–9) notes that in each stanza three couplets of four-stress lines with masculine rhyme are framed by two couplets of three-stress lines with feminine rhyme, and relates this to the sequence of tones which communicates 'the victory of the child's mind' as it advances from the first playful question to the final blessing. Gillham (1966, 243–5) sees the poem as 'a description of the world by a person who is protected', and points out that the speaker is 'delighted' to share his understanding of a God whom he knows as a 'constant companion'. Nurmi (1975, 62–3) deduces from the rhythms that Blake 'probably had music in mind', and locates the centre of the poem's harmony in the fact that 'child and lamb are united in the Incarnation and in the Agnus Dei'. Leader (1981, 87–91) observes that while the simple diction points to 'the child's way of seeing and speaking', we are also made 'to sense behind the child's lessons to the lamb the teachings of his parents'. Glen (1983, 23–5) compares the poem with Charles Wesley's 'Gentle Jesus, Meek and Mild', arguing that its lack of 'adult logic' articulates a 'deeply reassuring' teaching in which Wesley's hierarchies are 'subtly but surely dissolved'. Gardner (1986, 20–21) emphasises the way in which the 'firmly grounded' illustration 'transfers the divinity of the text' to a 'domestic, rural location, framed . . . in flourishing branches'. There is a large measure of critical agreement about the poem's success in conveying the innocent harmony promoted by the divine presence in the child, the lamb and the pastoral setting.

The miniature drama enacted in 'Nurse's Song' is concisely described by Hirsch (1964, 32 and 199–200). The opening lines define that 'reciprocity' which allows the nurse to benefit from the confidence expressed in the children's laughter. Her 'adult anxieties', awakened by the sunset, make her call out 'protectively', but in the ensuing disagreement she acknowledges the force of the children's arguments. The poem thus 'ends as it began', with the sounds born of this renewed trust being echoed by the natural environment. Erdman (1975, 65) finds the harmony between nurse and children confirmed in the design, where the playing children form a chain whose 'opening near the nurse includes her in the visual circle'. Leader (1981, 102–8) claims that the final tense-shift throws the action 'into an indefinite past', and that the design's 'abundant and energetic life' is qualified by the weeping willow of the right-hand margin. For Glen (1983, 20–23) both text and design suggest that the nurse has withdrawn 'into the stillness of contemplation', and that the children 'are moving into a world of which she will soon no longer be part'. Pointing out that the children's game is 'both spontaneous and organized', Gardner (1986, 28–9 and 43–7) stresses that their 'natural delight' arises from the knowledge that they have 'a home in humanity'; he invites us to recognise them as 'the infants from St James's, Westminster, sent out to nurse at Wimbledon, and well-known to Blake'. The mental drama of this apparently simple poem has evoked notably diverse responses from its many interpreters.

Keynes (1970, 137) declares that 'A Cradle Song' needs little comment because it 'conforms in its simplicity to the general pattern of all lullabies'; but other commentators have found it more complex and more problematic. Pinto (1944, 214–23) and others compare it with Watts's 'A Cradle Hymn', showing how Blake's subversion of syntactic order facilitates a merging of sensibilities appropriate to Innocence. The motif of 'interchangeable identities' is explored by Hirsch (1964, 30–31 and 190–91), who argues that while the mother sees Christ in her child, the poet sees Christ in the weeping mother. Gillham (1966, 182–90) notes that the mother finally ceases 'to distinguish carefully between the sounds and gestures expressed by the child and her own sympathetic responses'. Leader (1981, 97–102) attempts a sequential reading of the subtle and continuous changes in the mother's consciousness, showing how 'conventional distinctions between self and other' begin to dissolve as she slips away from 'the world of everyday reality'. Glen (1983, 135–6) argues that the speaker employs 'seemingly nonsensical, repetitive language' in order to construct through 'loving interaction with her child' a world 'which makes wider trust possible for both'. These interpretations reveal a common understanding of the text, but there is less agreement about the function and effect of the illustrations. For Gardner (1986, 58–60), the transition from the first plate to the second is in harmony with the poem's movement 'from a lullaby to a statement of faith'; but Leader (1981, 40–44) regards the 'unpleasant appearance' of the second plate as a critique of maternal affection and a warning that protection can tighten into possessiveness. It is hard to see, on either assumption, how the awkward contrast between the two plates can be an appropriate visual correlative for the conceptual and tonal unity of the mother's song.

Blake's visual artistry is more impressive in the two plates for 'The Little Black Boy', whose text is preceded by a picture of the maternal teaching the speaker remembers and succeeded by a vision of the paternal welcome which he foresees. The significant contexts of the poem include Blake's interest in Swedenborgian thought, whose relevance is explored by Raine (1969, I, 10–15), and his support for the anti-slavery movement, which is documented by Erdman (1954, 209–23). The poem seeks the attention of adult readers informed about such contexts, but invites them to share its impact on the English child-reader who is implicit in the book's generic conventions. Dyson (1959) notes how the impulse of tenderness flows from the mother through the speaker to the 'little English boy', and points out that while the conclusion is 'the very stuff of irony', its tone is neither ironic nor naive. Hirsch (1964, 179–81) identifies the mother's 'heathen myth' as an expression of 'the universal poetic-prophetic genius', and argues that the little black boy 'quite explicitly has Christ's role as intermediary between the little English boy and God'. Interpreting the poem as a critique of 'the social and religious attitude that made slavery possible', Nurmi (1975, 59–60) shows how the speaker first echoes and then transcends the value-system that 'takes whiteness to be the human norm'. Manlove (1977), claiming that most critics have failed to grasp the poem's 'powerfully dialectical and ironic character', demonstrates at length that the mother's theology is inconsistent. Leader (1981, 108–17) argues that the mother's 'confused and inadequate' teachings are reflected in the speaker's vision of eternity, and finds support for this view in 'unpleasant' features of the second plate. Though partly attributable to the colouring of some late copies, this reductive interpretation ignores major aspects of the poem's subtle and complex art. It is entirely typical of *Songs of Innocence* that the logical and linguistic discontinuities of this dramatic monologue should convey a perfect integrity of impulse, and that the speaker's unironic vision should serve as a vehicle for the poet's clearsighted attack on the psychological bases of injustice.

'The Chimney Sweeper'

This is the most complex of the dramatic monologues in *Songs of Innocence*, and has been the focus of much critical discussion. After borrowing a copy of *Songs of Innocence* from C.A. Tulk, Coleridge expressed himself 'perplexed' by this poem while declaring that 'Night' and 'The Little Black Boy' had given him pleasure 'in the highest degree'. Hazlitt 'preferred' it to the other songs Crabb Robinson read to him, but felt that it showed Blake to have 'no sense of the ludicrous' and that the songs in general were 'too deep for the vulgar'. In 1824 the poem was printed in *The Chimney Sweeper's Friend, and Climbing Boy's Album* by James Montgomery, who explained that it came from 'a very rare and curious little work' named *Songs of Innocence*, and had been 'communicated by Mr. Charles Lamb'. According to Alan Cunningham, the poem 'touched the feelings of Bernard Barton so deeply' that he wrote to Lamb asking about the author; and Lamb replied that if Blake was still alive he was 'one of the most extraordinary persons of the age'. Cunningham himself included a text of 'The Chimney Sweeper' in the account of Blake which he published in 1830 in his *Lives of British Painters*; and he declared the poem to be 'rude enough truly, but yet not without pathos'. Swinburne (1868, 115–16) reiterated Coleridge's preference for 'Night' and 'The Little Black Boy', but expressed his astonishment that 'The Chimney Sweeper', being 'so slight and seemingly wrong in metrical form', should 'come to be so absolutely right'. The growing admiration for Blake promoted first by Swinburne and W.M. Rossetti and then by Yeats and E.J. Ellis encouraged scholars after 1900 to interpret his lyrics in the light of his 'theories'. Berger (1914, 300) suggests that the 'black coffins' of 'The Chimney Sweeper' are intended 'to symbolise the soot-blackened bodies that imprison the pure innocent souls of these children'. Damon (1924, 269–70) observes that the children suffer silently 'even in the lowest degradation', and points out that the poem was 'actually used as propaganda' by those who campaigned 'against the use of children as chimney-sweeps'. Wicksteed (1928, 108–10) notes the ambiguity of the cry 'weep weep', and argues that it must have been 'a common sound in the morning streets of Blake's youth'. He suggests that Tom's vision arises from the 'Platonic thought' that his 'white hair' has been 'removed into a region of ideas', and contends that the word 'duty' in the seemingly 'trite and commonplace' final line must allude not to 'the sweeping of chimneys' but to 'the dreaming of dreams'.

Frye (1947) says nothing directly about 'The Chimney Sweeper', but his approach to Blake's work as a whole is a significant influence on most later commentaries. In his great study of Blake's relationsship to the 'history of his own times', Erdman (1954, 120) argues that the poem may have been written during the period of agitation which led to the 'protective' legislation of 1788. Bloom (1963, 42–3) argues that 'we need both to understand the limitations of the poem's dramatic speaker, and . . . to feel . . . the intensity of that speaker's Innocence'. Approaching the poem in this way, he claims that 'the child's illogic mounts to a prophetic and menacing sublimity', and that 'the final stanza . . . beats with a new fierceness . . . against the confining and now self deceiving trust of Innocence'. Seeing the poem as a 'canonical' statement of the values of Innocence, Hirsch (1964, 26–7 and 184–6) argues that its 'social protest is neither explicit nor angry', and that its 'didactic element . . . is directed to individual acts of Mercy, Pity, and Love'. In an important and informative article, Nurmi (in Frye 1966, 15–22) describes the conditions in which climbing boys lived and worked. He links the word 'sold' in the first stanza with the procedure by which the parents received a cash payment when a child was apprenticed to a master sweep, and points out that the phrase 'in soot I sleep' is not metaphorical, since climbing boys did indeed sleep 'on the bags of soot they had swept'. He connects the poem's 'coffins of black' with the narrow chimneys in which children sometimes 'got stuck and suffocated', and associates the nakedness of the children in Tom's dream with the fact that 'sweeps often went up chimneys naked, since clothes took up needed room'. Nurmi stresses that 'Blake deals with particular social evils symbolically in the comprehensive "prophetic" context of Innocence and Experience', but argues that a 'symbolic interpretation . . . that does not keep the cruel facts firmly in view is in danger of going badly astray'.

Gillham (1966, 38–44) offers a close reading of the poem in terms not of symbolism or social history but of its intricate dramatic strategies. Noting the speaker's 'explanatory' and even 'kindly' manner, Gillham attributes the comfort he offers Tom to a sense of the 'need for resolute action' which 'outweighs any sense of injustice'. He shows that while the angel's words are 'ugly' if taken out of context, the dream in which they are uttered is apprehended by the speaker in terms of its practical function in giving Tom a source of strength. While stressing the 'triteness and wrongness' of the words in the final line, he points out that they 'do really mean something' in the speaker's mouth, because the 'duty' to which he is committed includes an 'exercise of fellow-feeling' towards Tom. Gillham's reading identifies a major feature of the poem's dramatic method as a tactical ambiguity which at once exposes the origins and effects of cruelty and affirms the values of an Innocence that is 'neither ignorant nor naïve'. In a shorter commentary, Gardner (1968, 78–9) connects the name of 'little Tom Dacre' with 'the Lady Anne Dacre's Alms Houses' in St James's, and suggests that 'The Chimney Sweeper' is an application to the Westminster streets of 'the philosophy behind the poem *Night*'.

A new dimension of the poem is revealed by Raine (1969, I, 20–26), who cites Neoplatonic and Hermetic texts on the soul's transcendence of its corporeal prison, and stresses that dreams were for Blake 'states of real insight into the world of the imagination'. She quotes a remarkable passage of Swedenborg about 'Spirits . . . from the Earth Jupiter, whom they call Sweepers of Chimnies, because they appear in like Garments, and likewise with sooty Faces'. In one of his 'memorable relations', Swedenborg reported that one of these spirits had approached him 'in vile Raiment' and expressed 'a burning Desire to be admitted into Heaven', and that when 'the Angel called to him to cast off his Raiment' he had done so 'with inconceivable Quickness from the Vehemence of his Desire'. In this passage Raine finds evidence of a 'direct link between the chimney sweepers and Orc, who is Blake's Eros'. Her argument is supported and modified by Quasha (in Erdman and Grant 1970, 279), who points out that Swedenborg associated his 'Sweepers' with 'the Seminal Vessels', and that they 'illustrate exactly in their quickness and vehemence the correspondent quickness of seminal ejaculation'. The revelation of these metaphysical and erotic themes has influenced but not suspended discussion of the poem's dramatic and political strategies. In a study of 'the Development of Blake's Thought', Paley (1970, 32) argues that 'we are not led to endorse' the speaker's concluding statement, because while 'the innocence of the *speaker* is affirmed' the poet 'makes the reader feel what the speaker does not'. In his notes on the poem, Stevenson (1971, 68) reminds us that climbing boys often suffered from 'skin cancer caused by the soot which was literally never washed from their bodies'. Returning to the poem in his introductory book on Blake, Nurmi (1975, 61–2) relates it to a society which transforms children 'from white to black' and then 'finds warrant in their . . . blackness for viewing them as . . . sub-human'.

In a perceptive essay which goes some way towards reconciling these diverse readings, Glen (in Phillips 1978, 34–47) relates the poem's dramatic substance both to Jonas Hanway's humanitarian polemic and to Swedenborg's idiosyncratic allegory. In the monologue's leap from 'rational summary' to 'positive feeling for another', she sees the 'transforming power' of the speaker's 'unjudging responsiveness'; and in connection with the poet's ironic use of 'your' and 'all' she notes that while 'the sweep may be innocent . . . the target of the verse is not'. She cites evidence that the climbing boy's reputation was 'one of lawlessness and disorder', and suggests that the 'obvious sexual symbolism of his trade' made him 'a very potent image of subversive passion'. Noting that Tom's dream 'focusses on the release of *others*', she argues that the speaker 'activates a real truth' in the 'moral cliché, of the final line. In an undated issue of the Communist Party's literary journal *Red Letters*, Fauvet associates the 'Angel' in Tom's dream with 'the hypocrisy and repression practised in the name of the Christian religion', and asserts that the poem exposes Evangelical ideology by 'showing how it operates to incorporate the victims of oppression into the very structures that oppress them'. Reiterating the main arguments of her 1978 essay in her comparative study of Blake and Wordsworth, Glen (1983, 95–109) contends that in Tom's dream Blake is 'giving poetic articulation to impulses which the established official religion and morality of late eighteenth-century England sought to contain'. Crehan (1984, 66–7 and 102–3) inclines rather to Fauvet's view, identifying the 'moralising' Angel as 'Tom's own imprisoning trust', and claiming that the poem shows 'how comforting dreams of escape can actually reconcile us to our oppression'. A subtler interpretation is offered by Larrissy (1985, 13–34) in a contribution to the 'Rereading Literature' series edited by Terry Eagleton. While agreeing with Fauvet that the dream represents among other things 'the notion of ideology as a misunderstanding which favours dominant class economic interests', Larrissy points out that the dream not only ensures the maintenance of 'work discipline' but also mitigates the cruelty of Tom's existence. He acknowledges the poem's Swedenborgian dimension, and accepts Raine's claim that the sweep's soot may be 'the earthly mire and clay that cannot defile the spirit'; but he points out that Blake believed body and soul to be one, and argues that the Swedenborgian metaphor serves 'partly to impugn the cruelty and false hopes which such metaphors can sustain'. For Larrissy, the poem's vision is at once an 'exposure of Angels' hypocritical promises and dualist morality' and an affirmation of the 'happy communal state' implicit in the common humanity of the sweeps and the reader.

Transition and system

The developing concept of Innocence can be traced in Blake's work from the early shepherds' songs and the lyrics of *An Island in the Moon* to the great engraved book of around 1789 and the complex monologues for the little black boy and the chimney sweeper. In some of the lyrics that Blake engraved for the 1789 volume, however, the celebration of Innocence begins to modulate into a more explicit questioning of intellectual error and social injustice. The profound and complex changes which took place in Blake's mind and vision during the early 1790s had religious, political and sexual dimensions; and they found literary expression in printed and manuscript poems and in a series of non-lyrical engraved books. In this context the writing of additional lyrics for *Songs of Innocence* led naturally to the formulation of plans for a new engraved book in which the voices of Innocence would be answered by contrasting voices expressive of resentment, delusion, and prophetic indignation. By 1794 Blake was ready to engrave the title page for this new volume and the frontispiece and title page for its second part; and by about 1795 *Songs of Innocence and Experience* was an apparently completed work, although it still lacked 'To Tirzah'. The development of Blake's two-part scheme gave new substance to his conceptions of Innocence and its opposite, and provided a systematic framework for the creation of new plates and the reinterpretation of old ones. As he progressed with the major artistic and literary undertakings of his later career, his theoretical approach to the states of Innocence and Experience continued to develop within the context of his mythical and philosophical system; and that system, besides prompting the composition of 'To Tirzah', had some influence on the sequence and colouring adopted in late copies of *Songs of Innocence and Experience*.

Students of Blake are of necessity concerned with both the evolution and the intellectual coherence of his thought and art, and the conflicting demands of diachronic and synchronic analysis have occasioned some fruitful disagreements. The investigation of Blake's 'system' looms large in the work of E.J. Ellis and W.B. Yeats, and the 'system' they describe contributes something to Yeats's *A Vision* and to his later poems and plays. Berger (1914, 304–5) interprets the contrast between *Songs of Innocence* and *Songs of Experience* in essentially biographical terms, arguing that the poet 'has grown older', that his 'mental and spiritual point of view has entirely changed', and that his 'conception of childhood' has become 'less joyous'. Damon (1924, 39–44) provides an unstable bridge between biographical and systematic criticism by associating Innocence and Experience with the first two stages of the Mystic Way. Wilson (1927, 30–43) accepts this suggestion, but criticises Damon for imposing 'too systematic and definite a meaning upon the lyrics' in the light of his own reading of the 'symbolic books'. Wicksteed (1928, 25–6) judges it dangerous 'to elucidate early work by later, or a merely incipient symbolism by a far more developed one', and therefore makes less reference to Blake's 'system' in his commentary on the songs than in his commentary on the illustrations to Job. Besides offering a brilliant interpretation of the 'system' in its fully-developed form, Frye (1947, 237) argues that each state is satirised by the songs of the other, so that their opposition generates 'a double-edged irony, cutting into both the tragedy and the reality of fallen existence'. A vigorous attack on Frye's systematic approach is initiated by Hirsch (1964, 3–13), who emphasises the radical changes in Blake's thought, and claims that the poems of Innocence and Experience express 'two distinct outlooks that

Blake in each case held with an unqualified vigor and fervor of belief'. The systematic and anti-systematic approaches to Blake are not in the last analysis irreconcilable, since responsible study of his 'system' must involve some examination of its development; but in practice *Songs of Innocence and Experience* is interpreted very differently by those who read all the poems within the schematic framework offered by the late copies and those who read each poem within the context of Blake's thought and art at the time of its composition.

The differences between these approaches assume particular importance in relation to certain poems which anti-systematic interpreters regard as 'transitional'. The most obviously 'transitional' poems are those which were included in separate copies of *Songs of Innocence* but normally placed in the second part of *Songs of Innocence and Experience*: 'The Little Girl Lost', 'The Little Girl Found', 'The School-Boy', and 'The Voice of the Ancient Bard'. The first two of these compose a lyrical narrative occupying three plates, and have been interpreted by Raine (1969, I, 128–49) as a Blakean version of the Persephone and Demeter stories as enacted in the Eleusinian mysteries. As a representation of divine love's commitment to the generated soul, this narrative might seem closer to the paradisal vision of Innocence than to the revolutionary anger of Experience; but its effect is modifed by a two-stanza preludium in which the bardic narrator foretells a reawakening of the fallen earth as a transformation of the desert into a garden. 'The School-Boy' is a child-monologue like 'The Little Black Boy', but its rhetorical questions, like those of 'Earth's Answer' and the revised endings of *The Book of Thel* and *Tiriel*, express not transcendence but indignant complaint. Hirsch (1964, 291–2) reads it as an expression of 'Blake's incipient naturalism', and Gillham (1966, 211–14) observes that the speaker 'has an eye on the figure he cuts'. Leader (1981, 175–7) argues that 'the schoolboy's innocence seems compromised by the explicitness of its protest', and Gardner (1986, 107–8) observes that his reflections have 'an artificial gloss' and are voiced 'with assured poetic good breeding'. Responding more sympathetically to the speaker's complaints, Erdman (1954, 253) argues that Blake is concerned about the 'moral defeatism' imposed by 'the constraint of the classroom'; and he notes that the speaker in 'The Voice of the Ancient

Bard' has 'a contrary educational programme'. That poem, whose 'prophetic' manner is associated with a rhapsodically irregular verse-form, clarifies the significance of the bardic narrator in 'The Little Girl Lost'. The speaker, whose analogues include the bard of Gray's 1757 Pindaric ode, may be contrasted with the shepherd-piper in the 'Introduction' to *Songs of Innocence*; and Gleckner (1959) perceives the opposition between these two figures as a significant organising motif for *Songs of Innocence and Experience* as a whole.

Apart from 'To Tirzah' and the four poems transferred from *Songs of Innocence*, all but three of the poems in *Songs of Experience* were drafted in Blake's notebook when he was moving towards the two-part sequence. One of the exceptions, 'A Little Girl Lost', has a bardic preludium and may have been designed as a counterpart for 'The Little Girl Lost' and 'The Little Girl Found' before those poems were transferred. Wicksteed (1928, 160–70) considers it 'one of Blake's most important poems', and is prompted by it to a disquisition on 'Blake's theories of love and marriage'. Hirsch (1964, 279–81) identifies it as 'Blake's first unqualified poem of Experience', and takes from it the message that 'only artificial repression . . . prevents immediate and universal beatitude'. Another exception, 'Ah! Sun-Flower', is in itself a gently ironic critique of otherworldly aspiration; but it was reinterpreted to fit *Songs of Experience* by association with the notebook poems called 'My Pretty Rose Tree' and 'The Lilly'. The third exception, the 'Introduction', is linked to three of the transferred poems by the concept of a bardic summons to regeneration. Although this concept makes sense only in a postlapsarian context, text and design still maintain the compassionate harmony of Innocence; and the emergence of a harsher rhetoric in Experience thus prompted Blake to write and engrave a bitter sequel named 'Earth's Answer'. Because summons and response are visually as well as verbally discordant, the resultant symbolic drama is more obviously discontinuous than the symbolic narrative about the little boy lost and found; and refusal to acknowledge its discontinuity has sometimes obscured the subtlety of the 'Introduction' as a poem in its own right.

By asking precise questions about the participles and relative pronouns of the 'Introduction', Leavis (1936, 140–42) highlights an important series of syntactic ambiguities; but when he concludes merely that Blake's method 'disdains the virtues of prose', he ignores the function of those ambiguities in promoting significant identifications. Insisting that 'the serious reader' must ask 'whether the poem is a song of innocence or a song of experience', Gleckner (in Frye 1966, 8–14) contends that the bard is 'mortal but prophetically imaginative' and that the Holy Word is 'hypocritical, selfish, and jealous'. Seeking to interpret the poem 'in such a way as to make it an introduction to some of the main principles of Blake's thought', Frye (in Frye 1966, 23–31) relates it to Blakean theories about time, space, creation and resurrection; but his wide-ranging exposition communicates little sense of the poem's individuality. Paying homage to Frye as 'Blake's most distinguished commentator', Bloom (1963, 129–33) argues that the bard is 'limited by his perspective'; and this evaluation of Blake's persona allows him to show that the 'Introduction' and 'Earth's Answer' together announce 'the principal themes of the entire song cycle'. Identifying the Holy Word as 'both God and Adam', Beer (1968, 76–81) concludes that 'Earth and her Lord are mutually trapped', and that only the bard 'offers hope of a break in the vicious dialectic'. The desire for a perfect coherence in Blake's work often distorts and devalues its contradictory elements; and 'transitional' poems like the 'Introduction' are especially vulnerable to this kind of misreading.

Comparable problems arise over 'The Clod and the Pebble', the programmatic lyric which in many copies follows 'Earth's Answer'. Associating the clod with Innocence and the pebble with Experience, Damon (1924, 279–80) argues that while the clod 'has in it the germs of higher life' the pebble is 'completely dead'. Wicksteed (1928, 171–3) speaks of Blake's 'keen enjoyment of the pebble's ruthless honesty', and claims that the poem's argument is essentially that of *The Marriage of Heaven and Hell*. Hagstrum (1963) suggests parallels with 'other poems written out of disillusioning Experience', and insists that 'the Pebble, not the Clay, is Blake's *raisonneur*'. Claiming that Heaven and Hell are in this context 'strictly Swedenborgian', Raine (1969, I, 26–8) argues that the clod has the same status here as in *The Book of Thel*. Declining to choose between the poem's two voices, Glen (1983, 176–81) claims that its 'taut closure' exposes the 'sterile logic' implicit in a 'dichotomy between self and other' which places 'self-denial and selfishness' in 'hopeless deadlock'.

Counterparts

The earlier stages of the process which transmuted *Songs of Innocence* into *Songs of Innocence and Experience* can be followed in the 'transitional' poems and other works contemporary with them. Evidence for the later stages can be found in the notebook, where drafts of eighteen songs of Experience jostle with related verses which Blake never engraved. These eighteen poems, whose composition-sequence is discussed by Wicksteed (1928, 209–87) and Erdman (1973, 53–5), offer an expression and definition of Experience as Blake understood that state around 1792–5. Experience as a state of conflict and disintegration breeds a variety of moods and voices, from the self-centred to the prophetic; but the songs of Experience collectively map the postlapsarian realm which the songs of Innocence obliquely criticised. Lacking the harmony and integrity of Innocence, they stigmatise its idealism as gullibility; and the postlapsarian hypocrisies which they expose include the encouragement of Innocence as an exploitable condition. As the pastoralism of *Songs of Innocence* implied knowledge of a state other than Innocence, so the satiric method of *Songs of Experience* assumes familiarity with *Songs of Innocence* as statement of an ideal; and in *Songs of Innocence and Experience* the poems and designs of each part draw extra meaning from juxtaposition with those of the other.

Critical reactions to the Innocence–Experience antithesis are naturally affected by the dispute between systematic and anti-systematic interpreters. Writers wholly committed to the systematic approach relate every poem to the book's unifying scheme, which they see as a progression from Innocence through Experience to the 'higher Innocence' of 'To Tirzah'. On such an interpretation, the meaning of each poem is controlled by its function within the completed work; and the dramatic strategy establishes strict limits for the reader's imaginative assent to the values of either Innocence or Experience. Writers who claim more independence for the individual poems attain a perilous freedom of interpretation, which needs to be disciplined by scrupulous attention to each poem's original context; and they are also released from the system's restraining authority in respect of their responses to the 'two contrary states'. Many critics, being in this manner disinhibited, respond more strongly to one of those states than to the other; and the book's psychological dialectic is thus illustrated and continued in the conflicting opinions of its commentators. The ideals of Innocence are voiced by Hirsch in terms of Christian pastoral, by Raine in terms of Swedenborgian vision, and by Gardner in terms of caring and community. The perceptions of Experience direct the politico-historical reading of Bronowski, the humanist reading of Beer, and the Marxist readings of Aers, Crehan and Larrissy.

The problematic relationship between Innocence and Experience assumes its simplest form in those songs of Experience which were composed and engraved as parodic counterparts to particular songs of Innocence. 'Nurse's Song' takes three of its eight lines from the earlier poem of that title, but depicts not responsiveness and Edenic harmony but oppressive secrecy and resentment. For Bloom (1963, 134–5) this poem 'affords a remarkably instructive contrast to the first', in that it represents 'an existence both lower and higher, less and more real than the undivided state of consciousness'. For Hirsch (1964, 232–3) it is 'the most thoroughly parodic poem of *Experience*', and its exposure of the nurse's envious disillusionment is 'a satirical exemplum against the repression of natural instinct'. Though convinced that the vision of Innocence 'can, as yet, be realized only in an imaginary world', Aers (1981, 50–51) acknowledges that the nurse of Experience neither 'sees more truly' than her predecessor nor gives 'a more truthful account of the relations between adults and children'. Comparing the second nurse with the 'terrible Mrs Mason' of Mary Wollstonecraft's *Original Stories from Real Life*, Glen (1983, 20) suggests that the poem's exposure of her 'uncontrollable anxieties' is an oblique comment on the 'coercive admonitions' of eighteenth-century children's books.

'The Chimney Sweeper' presents as counterpart to the self-forgetful visionary of Innocence a sharp-witted child unforgivingly conscious both of his parents' treachery and of its ideological foundations. Recognising that this 'attack on *Innocence*' is conveyed with 'great compactness and telling irony', Hirsch (1964, 229–30) celebrates in particular the satiric logic implicit in its two parallel uses of the word 'because'. Gillham (1966, 44–8) interprets the child's tone as one of 'premature cynicism', and argues that he is 'too much involved in interpretation' and too quick to find 'motive and reason'. In a similarly hostile analysis, Leader (1981, 159–62) argues that the questioner's approach is 'calculated and manipulative' and that the 'analytical sophistication' of the child's reply sacrifices individual truth to generalised social argument. Responding more favourably to the child's 'unexpectedly powerful energies of expression and criticism', Aers (1981, 46–9) observes that the poem 'would seem to contradict' its precursor 'as truth contradicts illusion'; but he points out that while the poem of Innocence lacks 'critical perception' that of Experience lacks 'a vision of the future'. Gardner (1986, 111–13) suggests that the climbing boy of Experience is 'the son of a master sweep', and that his churchgoing parents are praising a God who has sanctified this 'profitable family arrangement'.

Whereas the 'Holy Thursday' of Innocence expressed the idealism of one who saw the annual charity-school service as a manifestation of loving care, the 'Holy Thursday' of Experience presents the horrified questions of one who recognises it as intolerable evidence of mass poverty in an affluent society. Making no distinction between speaker and poet, Hirsch (1964, 219) describes 'Holy Thursday' as 'an overly partisan and overly simple poem', and claims that it 'does not benefit on the whole by comparison with the poem it parodics'. Analysing the poem as a dramatic monologue, Gillham (1966, 192–7) observes that the speaker is 'so overcome by the awfulness of the problem' that he appears 'paralyzed . . . in the face of an injustice built into the fabric of society'. Aers (1981, 49–50) contends that the two 'Holy Thursday' poems 'raise the question of who sees truly', and that the answer 'heavily favours' the poem of Experience because it exposes 'the social condition which the spectacle of charity conceals'. Glen (1983, 170–76) analyses the speaker's 'withdrawal from actuality' and his inability to 'envisage a world different from that which he confronts'. Relating the poem to the 'demystificatory writings of Paine and his followers', she argues that Blake is here testing their thought 'against his own already realized vision of Innocence'.

'The Sick Rose', which is the counterpart in *Songs of Experience* for 'The Blossom' in *Songs of Innocence*, gives cryptic expression to the speaker's horror at the corrupting of the addressee by the worm of secrecy. Bloom (1963, 135) identifies the worm as 'the reasonable Selfhood that quests only to appropriate'; but he argues that 'the rose is not blameless', because her commitment to 'the self-enjoyings of self-denial' has caused 'the frustrations of male sexuality' to 'strike back'. Relating the poem to notebook verses on similar themes, Hirsch (1964, 89–91 and 233–5) identifies the rose as a woman whose 'outward show of modesty' promotes the 'repressive and hypocritical customs' of the father-god. Linking the worm with Milton's serpent and the storm with 'man's perversion of the natural order' in *King Lear*, he sees the poem as a 'naturalistic' interpretation of the Fall of Eve. Gillham (1966, 164–9) insists on the connection with 'The Blossom', and suggests that 'The Sick Rose' was perhaps meant 'as a satirical depiction of an unhealthy attitude to sexual love'. Gardner (1986, 145–8) connects the worm's 'secret love' with 'the moral code of the god of stealth', and finds in the poem 'a timeless compassion for our state of being'. Little attention has been given to the speaker of this enigmatic lyric, which is among other things a Blakean restatement of Adam's first speech to Eve after her Fall.

Whereas 'Infant Joy' celebrated the harmony of parents and child at the moment of conception, 'Infant Sorrow' declares the antagonism between child and parents at the moment of birth. In the notebook (Erdman 1973, N113) these two stanzas were the beginning of a longer poem (Keynes 1966, 166–7), but they acquired new meaning when Blake engraved them under a title which invited comparison with 'Infant Joy'. Hirsch (1964, 270–74) describes 'Infant Sorrow' as 'a highly affirmative poem', and claims that in embracing 'both the smiling and the screaming babe' Blake is proclaiming the 'rightness and divinity of actual life'. Gillham (1966, 180–82) points out that this poem like the second 'Nurse's Song' differs from its innocent counterpart in being a monologue without any hint of dialogue. Bronowski (1972, 160–61) suggests that Blake cut the notebook poem to eight lines because its 'whole progression' lay 'coiled in the first helplessness'. Glen (1983, 181–2) interprets the 'progressive waning' of the speaker's energy as a withdrawal into 'that egocentric selfconsciousness which was a central premise of eighteenth-century philosophy and science'. Gardner (1986, 125–8) recalls attention to the poem's literal and topical dimensions by citing eighteenth-century attacks on the practice of 'manacling' a newly-born child with swaddling clothes.

As 'A Dream' expressed the unselfregarding vision of a speaker in the state of Innocence, so 'The Angel' articulates the self-interested calculation of a speaker in the state of Experience. Hirsch (1964, 241–4) interprets the poem as an 'uncompromising satire' on the speaker's impercipient faith in 'the sanctity of childlike ignorance', and attributes the maiden queen's Fall to a repression of natural instinct which leads ultimately to the 'encrustation of Urizenic customs and habits'. Gillham (1966, 175–6) identifies the angel and the maiden queen with Cupid and Psyche, and offers a hesitant reading of the psychological progression from 'witless woe' to armed resistance. Keynes (1970, 148) describes 'The Angel' as a 'highly psychological poem' in which the poet 'imagines himself to be a woman dreaming of love'. Gardner (1986, 134–5) suggests that the dreamer's life is being 'telescoped into the inconsequential intimacy of a dream of virgin royalty', and that in this dream 'evanescent fulfilment breeds only tears and a tragic timidity'. These interpretations ignore the poem's relationship to 'A Dream', and fail to recognise the mental habits of Experience in the surprise and interrogation of the opening line. The speaker repeats in this negative response the self-involved rejection of love which has been symbolically re-enacted in the dream; and the poem thus effects an identification, not understood by the speaker, of both human and divine love with vision. This is a text which deserves more critical attention than it has so far received.

Voices of Experience

Pastoral and satire have been closely related throughout European literary history, and in *Songs of Innocence and Experience* they complement one another in a variety of ways. Satiric insights are at work in *Songs of Innocence*, but are communicated by the indirect strategies of pastoral. The pastoral ideal is a point of reference throughout *Songs of Experience*, but is enforced by satiric exposure of the negations which undermine it. A principal force behind the songs of Experience is prophetic anger, and this finds expression through a range of dramatic and polemical devices. An embittered speaker responds to the cruelties of fallen existence by remembering an Arcadian or Edenic realm which he has lost. An exuberant and imaginative child envisages an apocalyptic paradise whose implausible details condemn the society he inhabits. A worshipper of the sky-god claims to have destroyed his enemy by emulating the manoeuvres through which his idol brought about the Fall. An indignant visionary presents a grim drama of human sacrifice, and then invites us to recognise it as an allegory of power-relationships in contemporary Britain. An alienated wanderer observes in the streets of London the horrifying effects of the false ideology which promotes religious, political and sexual oppression. Critics may attempt to separate the metaphysical and social arguments in these affirmations of prophetic anger, but for Blake they are commonly aspects of a single meaning.

The speaker in 'The Garden of Love' connects his loss of Eden with the enforcement of prohibitive morality by an oppressive priesthood. Bloom (1963, 140) judges this 'the poorest of the *Songs of Experience*', and considers that it 'might perhaps have been better left in the notebook'. Hirsch (1964, 258–9) finds in it 'a confrontation between natural innocence and cunning repression', and argues that its account of 'a Fall from a garden to a graveyard' applies both to the speaker's history and to that of mankind. Seeing the poem as a Godwinian indictment of society, Gillham (1966, 177–9) describes its remembered paradise as 'a garden of self-indulgence', and claims that the priests' 'unhealthy repugnancies' are 'necessary checks to unhealthy impulses'. Leader (1981, 172–4) agrees that the speaker 'must himself bear some responsibility for what has happened', and contends that his attribution of blame to established institutions undermines that 'liberating power of vision' which was 'an essential truth of Innocence'. Glen (1983, 160 and 374) tentatively associates the poem with disputes in the Swedenborgian movement about 'the whole question of free love'. More convincingly, Gardner (1986, 139–41) connects its imagery with the building of a 'proprietary chapel' on 'land fronting South Lambeth Road'. Many critics have noted how the growing intensity of the speaker's anguish is enforced by imagistic and prosodic devices which culminate in the crucifixion-motif and amphibrachic rhythm of the last two lines.

The speaker of 'The Little Vagabond' is an outcast child who, being unwilling to accompany his mother to church, seeks to re-establish understanding by inviting her to share his extravagant fantasy about a socially-regenerative accord between God and the devil. Claiming that Blake is here 'at his most popular and most bitterly jovial', Bloom (1963, 140) argues that this poem 'spills more of the blood of the oppressive Church' than 'The Garden of Love'. Hirsch (1964, 259–61) contrasts the speaker's vision with the visions of Innocence, pointing out that his fantasy concerns a 'perfect happiness . . . in the actual world'. Gillham (1966, 198–201) acknowledges the truth of the child's 'attack on joyless religion', but argues that the poem's technique shows an 'untutored crudity' and that the child pursues 'very private and limited satisfactions'. Though he rejects this last phrase, Leader (1981, 172–4) considers that the speaker's acuteness is 'tricked out with the designedly endearing awkwardnesses of the *faux naïf* or child actor'. Gardner (1986, 115–18) observes that the poem's 'jaunty internal rhymes' contribute to a 'vagabond verse' which lacks 'proper deference to authority either parental or ecclesiastical'; and he provides useful evidence on the probable character of 'dame Lurch' and on the exclusion of poor people from services.

The artistry of this poem is more complex than its interpreters have so far recognised. It offers significant parallels and contrasts with 'The Little Black Boy', another child-monologue about motherhood and vision; and its erratic rhythms define the quickly-changing intonations with which the speaker persuades his mother to enjoy his escapist and therefore satirical fantasy. The child's desire for responsive love interacts convincingly with his sharp awarenesss of ill-treatment to create an apocalyptic daydream which communicates heartfelt longing with observant and sardonic wit. The subtle interplay of text and illustrations connects the speaker on the one hand with the devil's imagined reacceptance and on the other with adolescent alienation in a barren landscape. It is odd that Marxist critics have had so little to say about a poem whose speaker unites a critique of social injustice with advocacy of a classless society.

'A Poison Tree' is the self-congratulatory speech of one who has caused his enemy's death by strategies of concealment and temptation. Bloom (1963, 144) connects it with the Tree of Mystery in 'The Human Abstract', and describes it as 'a grisly meditation on the natural consequences of repressed anger'. Hirsch (1964, 274–6) notes that the speaker's disease appears more unnatural when 'described as a natural growth', and contends that the poem 'attacks the entire structure of a social order represented by the speaker and his foe'. Gillham (1966, 176–7) points out that the notebook draft is entitled 'Christian Forbearance', and argues that the speaker is not a 'dissembling hypocrite' but 'a man who is self-deceived'. Keynes (1970, 152) suggests that the poem 'shews how the repression of anger can breed malevolence, so that an artist such as Blake may rejoice in the downfall of a former friend who has stolen his ideas'.

Raine (1969, II, 32–48) relates the tree of this poem to other Blakean versions of the Tree of Mystery, and draws attention to the 'implicit analogy' between the speaker's behaviour and that of God in Genesis 1–3. Pursuing this line of argument, Gallagher (1977) suggests that the speaker's tale may be a mendacious account of a priestly murder. In a long and subtle analysis, Glen (1983, 187–98) relates the poem both to oral tradition and to Swedenborgian thought, and examines the process by which the tree comes to dominate a world that neither character can change. She explores the poem's links with the fabulous upas-tree of Java, which Blake had encountered in a work by Erasmus Darwin on which he worked as engraver; and she notes that 'the Poison-Tree of Java' appears in Swedenborgian literature as 'the *Tree of Death*, originating in *Hell*'. She compares the speaker's 'self-diminishing withdrawal from the human world' with clinical descriptions of the growth of schizophrenia and with Marx's account of the worker's alienation from his own activity; and she concludes that the poem 'delineates the coercive logic of those intertwined social and psychological strategies whereby men can imprison and destroy themselves and one another'.

Though it serves as counterpart to the story of the little boy lost and found, 'A Little Boy Lost' is more closely related to 'A Little Girl Lost', being concerned like that poem with a representative subjugation of natural impulse by prohibitive morality. Hirsch (1964, 276–9) explores the logic of the child's argument, tracing its epistemological origins and linking it with Blake's affirmation of natural energy as the divine substance. Gillham (1966, 83–9) claims that the boy does not know the implications of his words, and that the priest reacts not to their meaning but to the implied challenge to his status. Gillham sees 'no finesse . . . whatever' in Blake's attack on priestcraft, but argues that it avoids melodrama because the poet is 'conscious of the ridiculous'. Keynes (1970, 152–3) connects the last line with Blake's educational theory, reading it as a protest against 'the mental deformation caused by interference with the immature mind'. Leader (1981, 169–71) finds a conflict of themes in the poem, arguing that we are 'disturbed by the little boy's rationalism' but that the priest's violence 'embarrasses us into silence'. Gardner (1986, 109–10) claims that the boy's words reassert the values of Innocence and are thus 'a subversive threat to the ordering of society in Experience'. Although the discontinuities of its argument have aroused some interest, most critics find the poem's intellectual content less remarkable than its dramatic and rhetorical virtuosity.

'London', on the other hand, has commonly been recognised as a poem whose emotional power is controlled by a coherent vision. Interpreting it as a 'poem of concentrated wrath', Damon (1924, 283) points out that it is 'not only a protest' but also 'a picture of a mental state'. Wicksteed (1928, 190) notes the ironic force of the word 'charterd', whose positive connotations were being undermined by Paine. Erdman (1954, 255–8) cites evidence of republican slogans in St James's, and connects the rejected phrase 'german forged links' with the landing of Hanoverian mercenaries. Bloom (1963, 140–42) contends that the poem's political argument is contained within a 'larger apocalyptic impulse', and that the harlot is 'not just an exploited Londoner but nature herself'. Hirsch (1964, 262–5) argues that the poem's 'passionate irony' and 'uncompromising accusation' reflect 'Blake's revolutionary faith in a possible transformation of the human spirit'. Gillham (1966, 8–20) emphasises the poem's dramatic strategy, distinguishing between the 'forlorn mood' of the 'wanderer' and the 'steadier mind' that controls 'the imagery, the rhythm and the compactness of thought'.

Considering the poem as 'a profound analysis of human misery in cities', Johnston (in Erdman and Grant, 1970, 415–22) argues that it shows Blake's ability to make a 'genuine connection' between 'social alienation and personal alienation'. Glen (1976, 5–13) sees the persona of the 'lonely wanderer' as an acknowledgment that the poet 'is decisively implicated in his society', and argues that syntactic control is assumed in the latter stanzas by 'forces far more potent and overwhelming' than the isolated consciousness. Thompson (in Phillips, 1978, 5–31) investigates the biblical echoes in 'mark' and the multiple significance of 'bans', and argues that Blake's 'indictment of the acquisitive ethic' finds its 'necessary conclusion' in the harlot. Larrissy (1985, 42–55) relates the tensions within the poem to the fact that Blake could neither 'doubt the necessity of anger at injustice' nor 'trust that love would ever come out of anger'; and he attributes Blake's awareness of differing perspectives to the fact that he came 'from a radical Christian background in an age of radical rationalism'.

A Trilogy

Few critics would now wish to call Blake a symbolist poet, since his handling of symbols is markedly different from that of the French *symbolistes*; but the world inhabited by his mythical figures is defined through quasi-allegorical images of complex significance, and such images are no less important in his lyrical poetry. Some of them are examined by Gardner (1968, 41–60), who points out that a symbol's meaning is created and modified by the contexts in which it is used; and many critics have explored the intricacies of such major symbols as the rock and the tree. Flower-symbolism is of particular importance in *Songs of Innocence and Experience*, being connected with the Fall by the motif of the garden; and its traditional links with sexuality inform the text of 'The Blossom' and the design for 'Infant Joy', which are taken up in Experience by the plate for 'The Sick Rose'. King-Hele (1986, 35–61) relates this flower-imagery to that of Erasmus Darwin's *The Botanic Garden*, and points out that Blake's use of floral motifs to interpret human sexuality reverses 'Darwin's technique of humanizing the sexual activities of flowers'.

Flower-imagery is the obvious common feature in three songs of Experience which Blake chose to engrave on the same plate: 'My Pretty Rose Tree', 'Ah! Sun-Flower' and 'The Lilly'. 'My Pretty Rose Tree' is the first song of Experience in the notebook, where it appears untitled along with 'The Clod and the Pebble', 'The Garden of Love' and three unengraved lyrics expressive of sexual bitterness (Erdman 1973, 53 and N115). 'Ah! Sun-Flower' has a note of reproachful melancholy reminiscent of 'The Little Girl Lost' and the 'Introduction'; and though Stevenson (1971, 209 and 221) places it after the notebook poems, it seems likely that it was composed before them. 'The Lilly' appears untitled in the notebook six pages after 'My Pretty Rose Tree', along with 'Nurse's Song', 'London' and 'The Tyger'; and the same page has three unengraved fragments about jealousy and secrecy (Erdman 1973, 53–4 and N109). The manuscript evidence suggests that these three flower-poems were in origin separate from one another, and most critics have chosen to regard them as independent texts.

The speaker of 'My Pretty Rose Tree' is a husband who has rejected the opportunity for an extra-marital affair; he is distressed because his wife reacts to his dutiful loyalty not with

gratitude but with jealous irritation. Taking this story as autobiography, some critics have identified the 'sweet flower' as Mary
Wollstonecraft; but others insist on the poem's dramatic function
in *Songs of Experience*. Damon points out that Blake has extended
the tradition of the flower as 'symbol of sexual indulgence' by
representing the wife as 'a whole tree of flowers which may be
legally enjoyed'. Margoliouth (1951, 57–8) contends that the poem
was 'occasioned by . . . a marital misunderstanding', and links
this 'temporary trouble' with the period of 'continuous excite-
ment' that produced *Songs of Experience*. Gleckner (in Frye 1966, 8–9)
argues that the speaker has refused the opportunity for 'ascent to
a higher innocence', and that his enslavement to the marriage-
ring has made him retreat from desire into duty. Claiming that
the poem 'has the flavor of autobiography', Hirsch (1964, 253–5)
contends that it might not have been written if 'the intensity of
domestic frustrations had not called for a timely utterance'.

Praising the poem's 'subtlety of insight', Gillham (1966, 169–70)
argues that the speaker receives a 'well-merited snub' because his
false reasoning has revealed a 'proprietary' attitude to his wife.
Raine (1969, I, 217–18) refers to the speaker as 'the poet', but sees
his interest in the other woman as a 'symbolic reflection' of the
imagination's desire for 'some goal beyond any that is realizable in
terms of nature'. Stevenson (1971, 211) finds the autobiographical
reading 'plausible', but points out that there is 'no direct evidence'
outside the poem to support it. Glen (1983, 377–8) agrees that
the poem appears 'closer to a simple description of a personal
crisis than any of the other Songs', but goes on to demonstrate
that its psychological drama has polemical implications. Crehan
(1984, 115) summarises the poem as an 'indictment of bourgeois
marriage'. The 'loyal husband', seeking compensation for his
'missed opportunity', expects to enjoy 'the legal right of male
possession'; but his wife, the 'affronted yet conspiring victim of
a bonded relationship', declines to be treated as a 'passive sexual
object', and thus occasions his 'surprised yet knowing' expression
of self-pity. Gardner (1986, 143–4) whimsically suggests that the
'sweet flower' may have been the Blakes' neighbour Elizabeth
Billington, who was known as 'the Poland Street man-trap'.

'Ah! Sun-Flower' is a more problematic text, and has evoked a
greater variety of responses. Declaring this to be one of 'Blake's
supreme poems', Damon (1924, 281–2) interprets the flower as
a man who 'is bound to the flesh' but 'yearns after the liberty

of Eternity'. Bowra (in Bottrall 1970, 154–5) sees the flower as symbolic of all those 'who are held down to the earth despite their desire for release into some brighter, freer sphere'. Harper (1953, 139–42) argues that the poem was inspired by Thomas Taylor's *The Mystical Initiations; or, Hymns of Orpheus* (1787), and claims that it describes the aspiration of all 'natural things' to 'the sun's eternality'. Identifying the speaker as 'Blake himself', Bloom (1963, 139–40) reads the poem as an attack on the 'ascetic delusion', and argues that those who 'aspire only as the vegetative world aspires' undergo 'a metamorphosis into the vegetative existence'. For Hirsch (1964, 54–5 and 255–6) the poem conveys a longing for release both from the temporal world and from repression, and thus shows the author 'poised between the sacramental transcendentalism of *Innocence* and the revolutionary naturalism of *Experience*'. Gillham (1966, 209–11) identifies the theme as the wasting of life in otherworldly aspiration, and hesitantly defines the speaker's tone as a mixture of commiseration and amusement.

Keith (in Frye 1966, 56–64) associates the sunflower with Clytie in Ovid's *Metamorphoses*, and suggests that the youth and the maiden may be connected with the Narcissus and Persephone myths. Noting that the sunflower can be interpreted either as 'a straightforward image of aspiration' or as an ironic emblem of aspiration trapped in the natural cycle, Keith suggests that a full response to the poem should 'be able to hold both possibilities in suspension'. Developing and further documenting Harper's Neoplatonic reading, Raine (1969, I, 216–22) interprets the poem as a meditation 'on the theme of love as prayer'. Leader (1981, 167–8) finds it impossible to endorse either Bloom's 'pessimistic-sardonic reading' or Hirsch's 'unironic interpretation', and therefore supports Keith's plea that we should accept the poem's 'essential ambivalence'. Noting that all the images remain 'within the closed circle of subjective desire', Glen (1983, 185–7) relates this to the absence of a main clause and to the fact that all verbs indicating present activity 'describe a longing which never attains its object'. Observing that gardens are 'private places cultivated in Experience', Gardner (1986, 137 and 143) connects the poem's sense of 'aspiration unfulfilled' with the particularities of Blake's new surroundings in Lambeth.

'The Lilly', which Ellis called 'the most beautiful quatrain in the English language', is less obviously problematic than

'Ah! Sun-Flower'; but it too has evoked a remarkable diversity of interpretation. Damon (1924, 282) contends that the poem 'distinguishes between spiritual love and worldly love', and points out that the lily unlike the rose and the sheep 'fears nothing' and is willing to 'give her entire self'. Hirsch (1964, 256–8) contrasts the poem's ironic approbation of modesty and humility with its praise of uninhibited self-realisation. Gillham (1966, 174–5) argues that all three figures seek to attract love, the rose and the sheep by appearing to resist it and the lily by assuming a semblance of virginal ignorance. Raine (1969, I, 216–17) associates the lily with the Sophia, who was 'Adam's true love' before the creation of Eve. Leader (1981, 166–8) contends that these problems of interpretation 'ought not to be resolved, since they form part of a larger pattern in *Experience*'. A similarly ambivalent view is adopted by Glen (1983, 16–19 and 54), who argues that the poem has a 'teasing ambiguity' and that 'in its very refusal to point a moral it celebrates individuality and difference'.

As many critics have recognised, the poem's development can be traced in the notebook (Erdman 1973, N109), which indicates that the rose was first 'envious' and then 'lustful' before it became 'modest', and that the sheep was 'coward' before it became 'humble'. Blake's first version of line 4, 'And the lion increase freedom and peace', set the lion against the sheep as line 3 had set the lily against the rose; and his second version, 'The priest loves war and the soldier peace', was a crudely antithetical summary of the poem's aggressive paradox. These rejected readings place the ironic force of 'modest' and 'humble' beyond reasonable doubt, and show that the poem's origin lay in argument rather than emblem. They also highlight the rhetorical skill of the final text, where internal and terminal rhyme unite with anapaestic acceleration to confirm the lily's unaided victory over the rose and the sheep. Like many of the unengraved epigrams in the notebook, 'The Lilly' celebrates impulse and openness at the expense of hypocrisy and restraint; and it does so with an artistry that almost justifies Ellis's eccentric tribute.

Blake's decision to engrave these three poems on a single plate has received less attention than it deserves. Wicksteed (1928, 149–51) interprets the page as a 'diminutive' imitation of Dante, in which the first part represents 'transgression and pain', the second 'holy and purifying aspiration', and the third 'beatitude'. Raine (1969, I, 216) suggests that Blake 'intended the three to be read together' because in this order they offer 'a complete philosophy of love'. It has not been generally noticed that the motifs of self-delusion and disapproval connect the speaker of the first poem with the sunflower and the speaker of the second with the rose-tree. The contrast with the 'sweet flower' of the third poem is confirmed by the theme of possessiveness and alienation, which is visually represented in the design between the first poem and the second; and the engraved plate accentuates the word 'my' in the last line of 'My Pretty Rose Tree', which is echoed or reciprocated in the last line of 'Ah! Sun-Flower'. The large narrative condensed on this page seems less an eschatological vision than a Lawrentian fiction.

Part Two:
Appraisal

Novitiate: 'Holy Thursday'

Appreciation of *Songs of Innocence and Experience* has been advanced by scholarship and criticism of many kinds: the editions of Keynes and Erdman, the poem-by-poem commentaries of Wicksteed and Hirsch, the work of Damon and Frye on Blake's philosophy and symbols, Nurmi's investigation of the sociohistorical context and Raine's quest for Swedenborgian and Neoplatonic sources, Gardner's recreation of Blake's physical surroundings and Larrissy's analysis of his ideological stance. Interpretations which at first seem incompatible often prove on closer examination to be complementary; and the best recent contributions, such as Glen's reading of 'A Poison Tree', achieve a depth of understanding at which differing perspectives are convincingly reconciled. The writer who can tell us most about *Songs of Innocence and Experience*, however, is still Blake himself; and because the book's composition was spread over three decades at the height of his career, a high proportion of his literary and artistic work is in some sense contemporary with it. Since Blake continually revised and developed his vision, one must always be wary of interpretations derived from his later inventions; but the relative chronology of Blake's writings is now sufficiently understood for each poem to be considered in the light of earlier and roughly contemporary texts. Adopting this approach, one finds that apparently simple poems like 'The Ecchoing Green', 'The Tyger' and 'To Tirzah' are often illuminated by obviously difficult poems like *The Book of Thel*, *The Song of Los* and *The Four Zoas*.

Blake was born in London on 28 November 1757, and was baptised in St James's Church, Piccadilly. He was the son of James Blake, a 'hosier and haberdasher' living at 28 Broad Street near Golden Square. On 4 August 1772 he began, under the topographical and antiquarian engraver James Basire, a seven-year apprenticeship during which he probably lived with Basire's family at 31 Great Queen Street in Lincoln's Inn Fields. Basire's clients included the Society of Antiquaries, and from 1774 onwards Blake was regularly employed on sketching the Gothic tombs in Westminster Abbey. His literary interests of this period are reflected in the juvenile poems later collected and printed as *Poetical Sketches* (Keynes 1966, 1–40). These include prose-poems influenced by Macpherson and Gessner, dramatic fragments modelled on Shakespeare's histories, ballads and lyrics resembling those in Percy's *Reliques*, and mythopoeic verses in the manner of Collins' odes. They reflect a fashionable taste for Spenser, Milton and other pre-Augustan authors; and two at least offer visions of rebellion against tyranny which were clearly inspired by the American War. Imitative as they are, they show the young engraver to have a talent both for dramatic lyric and for mythical narrative; and his interest in these modes is further expressed in other juvenile works which have survived, such as the pastoral lyric which later became 'Laughing Song' (Keynes 1966, 63) and the mythical prose-poem which begins 'then she bore pale desire' (Keynes 1966, 40–43).

Blake presumably finished his apprenticeship in August 1779; and on 8 October he was accepted as a student at the Royal Academy of Arts, where he met and disliked Sir Joshua Reynolds. On 6 June 1780 he witnessed the storming and burning of Newgate Prison during the Gordon Riots; and in September 1780, while sketching on the Medway with Thomas Stothard and others, he was briefly arrested as a suspected French spy. On 18 August 1782 he was married at St Mary's Church in Battersea to Catherine Boucher or Butcher, the uneducated daughter of a market-gardener. He read and sang his poems at Harriet Matthew's salon in Rathbone Place, where they were 'allowed by most of the visitors to possess original and extraordinary merit'; in 1783 a collection of them was privately printed as *Poetical Sketches*, and his friend John Flaxman sent a copy to the Whig poet William Hayley. Blake had exhibited a historical picture at the Royal Academy in 1780; and in 1784–5 he exhibited six drawings, one of them an illustration to Gray's 'The Bard'. After his father's death in 1784 he joined with his former co-apprentice James Parker in opening a printselling business next door to his birthplace; and he may at this time have acquired a copperplate press. The partnership was shortlived, however, and by Christmas 1785 the Blakes had moved to 28 Poland Street. In February 1787 Blake's favourite brother died at the age of nineteen. According to stories repeated by his Victorian biographer Alexander Gilchrist, the poet saw 'the released spirit ascend heavenward through the matter-of-fact ceiling'; and some time later Robert appeared to him 'in a vision of the night' and revealed 'the technical mode by which could be produced a fac-simile of song and design'.

Blake's main surviving literary work of the years 1784–7 is the untitled fragment of prose satire commonly known as *An Island in the Moon* (Keynes 1966, 44–63). This is a cryptic and disorderly piece which can scarcely have been designed for publication; but it surpasses most of *Poetical Sketches* in its philosophical wit, its realistic and surrealistic energy, and its variety of mood and style. Its social world, though treated with ludicrous extravagance, is manifestly that of the author's immediate environment; and its absurdly-named characters, whom Erdman and others have laboured to identify, must have been immediately recognisable to members of Blake's circle. The most penetrating satire is directed at the Cynic, the Pythagorean and the Epicurean, who represent the author and two close associates. Other figures, such as Etruscan Column and Inflammable Gass, are broadly caricatured like the dupes in Jonsonian comedy; and one of these is Obtuse Angle the mathematician, whose entry in Chapter 1 averts an imminent quarrel.

With a Sternean attention to gesture, Blake tells us that Obtuse Angle 'turned about and sat down, wiped his face with his pocket handkerchief, and shutting his eyes, began to scratch his head'. When his first conciliatory question evokes solipsistic replies from the philosophers, he responds with a self-deprecating grin; and when the 'Wind-finder' becomes aggressive he reacts by claiming that he always understands better with his eyes shut. Even a rude interruption from the Epicurean merely causes him to scratch his head with double violence and say, 'It is not worth Quarreling about'. Chapters 3 and 5, whose analysis of schooling anticipates the Mad Hatter's tea-party, show Obtuse Angle as an incompetent instructor whose benevolent pedantry reduces his pupil to babbling confusion; but in Chapter 8 he corrects both the vagueness of Steelyard and the lumpish ignorance of Scopprell, and in Chapter 9 we find him 'wiping his face and looking on the corner of the ceiling' while he celebrates the founder of Charterhouse. He praises Thomas Sutton in preference to Locke, South, Sherlock or Newton because Sutton devoted his property and energy to the practical purpose of building a house for 'aged men and youth', and because he ensured that it was well supplied with chimneys, windows and drains to 'hinder pestilence'. Obtuse Angle is depicted as a naive and kindly man who dislikes acrimony and does not aspire to philosophical sophistication; and it is he, after the pestilence-releasing explosion of Chapter 10, who responds to Miss Gittipin's invitation with a song which makes the company sit 'silent for a quarter of an hour'.

No-one who remembers Uncle Toby should be surprised that Blake's Shandean fragment allows a comic altruist to articulate its highest vision. The lyrical power of Obtuse Angle's song carries us beyond Sternean sentimentalism, however, into a poetic and authoritative affirmation of the singer's integrity. In the manuscript of *An Island in the Moon* we can see Blake working for this effect, eliminating the controlling authority of the 'chief chanter' and the false sublime of the 'Cherubim and Seraphim'; and if we compare the manuscript text with 'Holy Thursday' as engraved for *Songs of Innocence*, we can see the effect being enriched by further emendations, like the replacement of 'grey' with 'red' in line 2. Much of the song's emotional power, however, arises from the lyrical impetus of its riverlike fourteeners, whose processional music is taken up in the engraved design by the extended processional images above and below the text.

'Holy Thursday' describes in biblical language and through the eye of Innocence the annual procession to St Paul's of between four and five thousand London charity-school children. This spectacle moves the speaker to a wonder which registers the column as ordered and yet natural, which delights in the pure colours of the uniforms and the beadles' staffs, and which follows the children into the cathedral with a sense of fulfilment. The second stanza describes the scene within, seeing the children's scrubbed faces as flowers of the city, hearing their murmuring voices as the bleating of lambs, and interpreting the raising of their hands in prayer as an expression of their joy in the loving kindness that has rescued them from starvation. In the third stanza their singing becomes the mighty harmony of the heavenly choirs, and through their place in the dome they assume the role of angelic protectors over those who shepherded them to the service. The last line defines the lesson as understood by the innocent speaker: that pity reveals the divine presence in those to whom it is extended. The worldly-wise reader, like the philosophers in *An Island in the Moon*, may see harsh implications to which the naive visionary's eyes are closed: this ceremony is the result of poverty in the midst of prosperity, the double line and the uniforms are evidence of regimentation, the beadles' 'wands' are frequently used for punishment, London is cruel to flowers and lambs, and the 'guardians of the poor' are often lacking both in pity and in wisdom. But the speaker's unembittered vision demands that we should exercise, in the manner suggested by our superior knowledge, a love comparable to that which his Innocence believes to be manifest in this assembly.

Those critics who see the predominant sense of this poem in its satirising of the speaker's naivety are not only resisting the overwhelming force of its rhythms and its imagery; they are also protecting themselves against the challenge of its vision by acknowledging only the subordinate and less disturbing portion of its political argument. A knowledge of the poem's origins in Blake's Sternean novel is by no means necessary to an appreciation of its verbal and visual effect; but it can help to clarify our understanding of the dramatic and poetic strategies by which that effect is achieved.

Eden: 'The Ecchoing Green'

Some time in 1788 Blake perfected the new method of printing which his dead brother had revealed to him; and from then onwards most of his writings were reproduced by this process. The earliest known example is a sequence of ten minute and rather clumsy plates with the general title *All Religions Are One* (Keynes 1966, 98; Erdman 1975, 24–6). The seven 'Principles' which contain the main substance of this work identify the primary faculty as the 'Poetic Genius', affirm that it has the same basic form in all men, and conclude that all religions, being derived from the 'universal Poetic Genius', must be essentially one. This pseudo-logical tractate was followed by two comparable but technically superior sequences, each of which bears the general title *There Is No Natural Religion* (Keynes

1966, 97–8; Erdman 1975, 27–32). The first sequence argues that rational interpretation of sensory evidence could of itself produce only 'natural and organic thoughts', and that the 'Philosophic and Experimental' character is therefore dependent on the 'Poetic or Prophetic'. The second affirms that man's perceptions and desires are not circumscribed by the senses, and draws the conclusion that 'God becomes as we are, that we may be as he is'. The repudiation of Lockean psychology thus opens the way for a celebration of the Poetic Genius as incarnate divinity.

The implications of these tractates are clarified in Blake's annotations to his friend Fuseli's translation of Lavater's *Aphorisms on Man* (Keynes 1966, 65–88). When Lavater describes 'the saints of humanity' as 'heroes with infantine simplicity', Blake declares this observation to be 'heavenly'; and in response to Lavater's apologia for his work, he observes that a man should not take offence at 'the innocence of a child' when it reproaches him with 'the errors of acquired folly'. When Lavater states that 'a god, an animal, a plant are not companions of man', Blake insists on the contrary that 'it is the God in *all* that is our companion and friend'; and after quoting St John's statement that 'whoso dwelleth in love dwelleth in God and God in him', he adds that 'such an one cannot judge of any but in love'. Though he speaks of man as 'a twofold being' capable of both evil and good, Blake asserts nonetheless that 'human nature is the image of God'; and he argues that vice is always negative, and rejects the notion that 'Woman's Love is Sin'. Erdman (1954, 116–17) rightly describes these annotations as 'the nearest thing we have' to an authorial commentary on *Songs of Innocence*.

By the winter of 1788–9 Blake had become deeply interested in the Swedenborgian movement; and on 13 April 1789 he and his wife attended a general conference of the New Jerusalem Church and signed a paper endorsing Swedenborg's doctrines. Resolutions adopted on this occasion condemned the idea of a three-person Trinity and declared that the creator 'came down himself to remove Hell from Man'. Blake's contradictory feelings about the movement are reflected in his annotations to the 1788 edition of Swedenborg's *Divine Love and Divine Wisdom* (Keynes 1966, 89–96), which were probably written soon after the conference. Many sentences are annotated with approving phrases like 'Mark this' and 'Excellent', and there are other comments which merely restate Swedenborg's arguments in more emphatic terms; but elsewhere the annotator seems rather to contradict his author. When Swedenborg asserts that 'the Lord, although he is in the Heavens with the Angels everywhere, nevertheless appears high above them as a Sun', Blake replies that 'He who Loves feels love descend into him and if he has wisdom may perceive it is from the Poetic Genius, which is the Lord'.

The world-view defined in the tractates and in these annotations to Lavater and Swedenborg was given literary expression around 1789 in a mythical narrative-poem entitled *Tiriel* (Keynes 1966, 99–110), which describes the death of an aged monarch resembling Oedipus and Lear. In presenting the downfall of Tiriel's ancient empire through his encounters with other mythical figures, the poem reveals that his godlike authority is the product of humanity's retreat into a factitious paradise. A longstanding disorder of the individual and collective psyche is thus attributed to the imagination's wilful subservience to the uncreative reasoning power, whose enthronement has promoted an era of tyranny and delusion. The last of the poem's eight sections was rewritten some time after composition, and therefore reflects the development of Blake's thought in the early nineties. The story of Tiriel's downfall and death is told in unrhymed seven-stress lines, and is reflected in a series of pictures separate from the manuscript. These pictures and other evidence suggest that Blake may have hoped for a printed edition with full-page illustrations, but in fact *Tiriel* was neither printed nor engraved during his lifetime.

A complementary story is presented in *The Book of Thel* (Keynes 1966, 127–30; Erdman 1975, 33–41), a shorter narrative-poem also in unrhymed seven-stress lines, which Blake produced as an engraved book with the date 1789 on its title page. The central figure here is the shepherdess Thel, who voices her gentle discontent in dialogues with the lily-of-the-valley, the cloud and the clod of clay, and transcends her self-involvement in response to the vulnerability of the worm. The manner in the first three chapters is not tragic and imperial but pastoral and naively didactic; and the subject is at once the soul's descent into material existence and the virgin's dawning awareness of sexuality. Like *Tiriel*, the poem was transformed some time after its composition, when Blake rewrote its final section from a less innocent standpoint; and the paradoxical relationship between its two perspectives then prompted a prefatory quatrain entitled 'Thel's Motto', which offers a cryptic challenge to the interpreter. Different as they are both in atmosphere and in method of production, these two narratives reflect both the ideology and the developing vision of the months in which Blake was engraving *Songs of Innocence*. The exact chronology of the three books is uncertain, but all three must have been substantially advanced before any one of them achieved a definitive shape.

Four of the lyrics in *Songs of Innocence* can be identified as early because they survive in dateable manuscripts, and another four as probably late because they were subsequently transferred to *Songs of Experience*. We have little evidence concerning the dates of the other fifteen, but can plausibly associate their engraving with that of the title page in 1789. The most obviously programmatic of them, apart from the 'Introduction', are 'The Divine Image' and 'On Another's Sorrow'; and in these we can recognise lyrical and dramatic affirmations of the doctrine of incarnation as it was defined in the tractates. Such poems as 'A Dream' and 'The Lamb' are among other things poetic realisations of the principle, stated in the annotations to Lavater, that one in whom God dwells 'cannot judge of any but in love'. The gentle idealism of 'A Cradle Song' and 'Night' invites comparison with Thel's comfort-seeking dialogues; and the Darwinian flower-imagery of the title page for *The Book of Thel* casts some light on the text of 'The Blossom' and the design for 'Infant Joy'. On the other hand, the pastoral strategy of poems like 'Spring' and 'The Shepherd' assumes that the reader has experienced the psychic and social disorders represented by Tiriel's empire; and the cruelty and hypocrisy occasioned by those disorders are threatening presences behind the speakers of 'The Chimney Sweeper' and 'The Little Black Boy'.

Approaching 'The Ecchoing Green' from Blake's other writings of 1788–9, one sees at once that it celebrates a communal harmony renewed by mutual responsiveness among beings in whom divinity is incarnate; and one recognises also that it achieves, perhaps on some basis of personal experience, a physical immediacy which recalls lines 15–34 of Goldsmith's *The Deserted Village*. The title identifies the meeting-place by the oak as an Eden of growth and security, whose echoes testify like those of 'Nurse's Song' both to uninhibited youthful energy and to a seamless web of reciprocity and interinvolvement. The pattern of echoes involves the sun and the skies, the bells and the spring, the birds and the children's games; and the curious syntax of line 9 seems to identify the last of these as the activating force of the poem's natural world. The echo-motif is taken up in the old people's recollections, in the variable refrain, and in a carillon of repeated monosyllables: bells, old, laugh, such, seen, sun, sports, birds. The inclusiveness of this localised harmony is stressed by the presence of all age-groups, so that the poem conveys a sense of the process by which communal values are renewed from generation to generation. The many intimations of time and mutability cause neither fear nor resentment, being apprehended only as they direct the particulars of empathy and creative impulse; and the linear progression is answered by a cyclical movement which associates the rhythms of human life with those of the day. The cyclical scheme is subtly enforced by prosodic variation, the change of direction in stanza 3 being signalled by the feminine rhymes of 21–2 and 25–6 and confirmed by the initial iambs of 28–9.

Both linear and cyclical forms are prominent in the designs, which endorse the text's celebration of communal harmony but offer stronger hints of the forces that can undermine it. The large picture on the first plate shows the generations at play around a massive oak, but connects that tree with ambiguous images of enclosure; and in the smaller designs a boy with a bat looks across the text at another who is rolling a hoop into the next page, while beneath them a swallow-like bird swoops on a bunch of grapes. The large picture on the second plate shows adults and children moving amicably homeward, with old John pointing ahead and the young batsman looking up to him; but a different mood is apparent in front of them in the youth carrying a kite and behind them in the adolescent girl whose hat looks like a halo. As the youth looks back regretfully and perhaps jealously, the girl reaches up to accept a bunch of grapes from a figure reclining in the upper branches; and to the left of the text, still further beyond the old man's range of vision, a similar figure is stretching towards a larger bunch which seems just out of reach. These designs, much more than the poem, foreshadow the coming movement from Innocence to Experience.

Generation: 'The Little Girl Lost' and 'The Little Girl Found'

It is a significant feature of Blake's literary development that he often becomes dissatisfied with his own thoughts and writings almost before he has formulated them. Such dissatisfaction expresses itself in self-parody, in the continual re-fashioning of mythical characters, in the ironic use of words previously used unironically, in sequels which reinterpret the works they continue, in the insertion of new material into completed texts, and in attempts to change almost-completed poems in accordance with new ideas. These procedures are especially prominent in Blake's work of the early nineties, where they are associated with profound and complex changes in his beliefs, his vision and his art.

One readily-identifiable element in this process of change is the virtual reversal of Blake's attitude to Swedenborg. Whereas the annotations to *Divine Love and Divine Wisdom* expressed qualified admiration, those to the 1790 edition of *Divine Providence* (Keynes 1966, 131–3) are decisively hostile. Closely related to Blake's rejection of Swedenborg is a dramatic change in his perception of incarnate divinity. The God worshipped by the churches is now exposed with growing vehemence as an agent of tyranny and repression, and Christ's redemptive power is increasingly connected not with Innocence but with a fiery and rebellious energy. The celebration of energy has sexual implications, being linked with free love and with the denunciation of that prohibitive ideology which Blake calls the Female Will. The rebel-tyrant antithesis, which recalls Blake's poems of the American War, serves as vehicle for an aggressive proclamation of political radicalism in the context of London responses to the French Revolution. These changes in Blake's religious, sexual and political attitudes find expression especially in his engraved books of the early nineties, which show a new boldness and aggressiveness both in language and in design; and they must in some measure have been promoted by his contact with the radical bookseller Joseph Johnson, whose intellectual circle included Henry Fuseli, Mary Wollstonecraft and Tom Paine. The connection with Johnson was no less profitable in material terms, bringing commissions for the plates to such works as Stedman's *Narrative of a Five Years' Expedition in Surinam*; and Blake's modest prosperity as an engraver enabled him to move late in 1790 to a house with a garden at 13 Hercules Buildings in Lambeth.

Blake scholarship has not yet determined the exact sequence of composition for his various writings of the early nineties; but the transmutation of his art and outlook can be examined in a number of works probably written between the storming of the Bastille in July 1789 and the execution of Louis XVI in January 1793. The harshly rhetorical speech which dominates the revised ending of *Tiriel* (Keynes 1966, 109–10) asserts an educational theory like that of 'The School-Boy' and 'The Voice of the Ancient Bard'; but it is also linked to 'Thel's Motto' by the enigma of the rod and the bowl, and to *The Marriage of Heaven and Hell* by the aphorism about the lion and the ox. Chapter 4 of *The Book of Thel* (Keynes 1966, 130; Erdman 1975, 40) gives a still fiercer account of man's entombment in the torture-chamber of the senses; and by answering Chapters 1–3 as Experience answers Innocence, it transmutes a gently didactic children's story into a painful drama of conflicting ideologies. *The French Revolution* (Keynes 1966, 134–48), which was printed for Johnson as the first book of 'a poem in seven books', reshapes Parisian events of 1789 into a revolutionist vision which owes something in substance to *Paradise Lost* and something in style to Macpherson's Ossian.

Blake's amplest and most eloquent exposition of his new ideology is the engraved book in 27 plates which he called *The Marriage of Heaven and Hell* (Keynes 1966, 148–60; Erdman 1975, 97–124). Apart from the opening 'Argument' and the concluding 'Song of Liberty', this work is in prose; and though it effects a critique of eighteenth-century thought, it is among other things a parody of Swedenborg in the eighteenth-century satirical tradition. After a title page which represents a subterranean union of Heaven and Hell as the source of vital energy on earth, the book opens with a cryptic passage of irregular verse entitled 'The Argument'. The unfallen world is here recalled as a time of fertility associated with the just man's presence in the 'perilous path'. The Fall is described as an expulsion of the just man by the villain, a 'sneaking serpent' who professes 'mild humility'; and the just man's accumulated anger is manifest in the storm-clouds of imminent revolution. After this mythical opening, the book advances through an alternation of theoretical and imaginative statement. First we have a sequence of paradoxes and loaded definitions which links Heaven with reason and Hell with energy; and then, under the heading 'The Voice of the Devil', we have an aphoristic assertion of the infernal belief in the superiority of energy to reason. This belief is supported by archetypal readings of *Paradise Lost* and Job, which equate the Messiah of the former work with the Satan of the latter; and then, under the Swedenborgian heading 'A Memorable Fancy', the author like a good anthropologist offers a selection from the proverbs of Hell as evidence on the character of its society.

Through this alternation of extravagant theory and fantastic narrative, which continues on plates 11–24, Blake's audacity and inventiveness build up a fund of imaginative energy; and in the concluding 'Song of Liberty' that energy is released in a celebration of the Atlantic Revolution. Instead of the short, tense lines of the 'Argument', the 'Song' offers long, sweeping verses; and the revolution it envisages is seen not only as a transformation of religious, political and economic life but also as the successful rebellion of a fiery child against the 'gloomy king' and his 'starry hosts'. The 'Song' culminates in an ecstatic 'Chorus' with the ending 'For every thing that lives is holy'; and that ending finally rejects the values Blake attributed at the outset to 'Heaven'. *The Marriage of Heaven and Hell* presents neither a coherent narrative nor a logically sequential argument; but its progression from imminent revolution through alternating theory and fancy to revolutionary triumph does nonetheless give it a satisfying artistic shape. The much-quoted aphorisms, such as the proverbs of Hell and the interpretation of Milton, should be seen in the context of Blake's satirical and polemical strategy.

The revolutionist ideology proclaimed in the satirical prose of *The Marriage of Heaven and Hell* forms the intellectual basis for seven mythopoeic engraved books, all of which have title pages dated 1793, 1794 or 1795. *Visions of the Daughters of Albion* (Keynes 1966, 189–95; Erdman 1975, 125–36), which differs from the others in not specifying Lambeth as place of publication, is almost certainly the earliest; and its connections with Blake's engravings for Stedman suggest a composition-date of late 1791 or early 1792. The title identifies the substance of the poem as a series of visions in which the women of Britain recognise a mythical definition of their oppressed condition; and the poem proper is divided into three sections by short allusions to the Daughters of Albion as choric visionaries responding to its characters and events. The magnificent frontispiece, however, focuses attention on the three major figures of the poem's mythical narrative, whom Blake calls Theotormon, Oothoon and Bromion. Theotormon, as his name indicates, is an individual or collective sensibility disordered by the worship of suffering: in a later poem he is connected with Jesus as 'a man of sorrows', and Blake's presentation of him is a radical critique of traditional Christian morality. This misdirected worship is a withdrawal from the integrated humanity of Eden, and its consequences include the separation of female from male and the perversion of frustrated instinct into a negative and destructive power. The creation of Eve as a being distinct from Adam was an aspect and emblem of the Fall; and Satan was not the causer of that Fall but a monstrous hallucination produced by it. In the psychic drama of these visions, the relationship of Oothoon and Bromion to Theotormon is that of Eve and Satan to Adam; but the loss of Eden is attributed not to Oothoon's impulsive plucking of the flower but to Theotormon's false perception of that act as sinful. In her commitment to love and her persistent summons to reintegration, Oothoon is a libertarian embodiment of Christ's redemptive energy; and as such she denounces the prohibitive ethos of the 'gloomy king', who is here named for the first time as Urizen.

The series of notebook poems which includes drafts of eighteen songs of Experience (Keynes 1966, 161–88; Erdman 1973, N101–15) was probably written soon after *Visions of the Daughters of Albion*, during a relatively short period which ended soon after 25 October 1792. Being predominantly lyrical and epigrammatic, the unengraved notebook poems reflect Blake's new attitudes in more obviously personal ways; and in this context we can see the Innocence–Experience dialectic emerging not from theological or political argument but rather from sexual anxiety and the repudiation of dogma. A recurrent motif in these poems is the woman who prefers an assertive or deceitful suitor to one who is honest, articulate and humble. This apparent injustice moves the poet to romantic lamentation, self-mockery, philosophical irony, sexual revulsion, and rhetorical protest against the 'gloomy king'; and it also provides the stimulus for a critical analysis of that received system of morality which advocates modesty and self-denial instead of valuing uninhibited life. Such an analysis is effected through dramatic monologue, through parody of *Songs of Innocence*, through the myth of the power-seeking fairies, through denunciation of the cult of pity as a cult of suffering, and through the symbolism of sun and wind, barrenness and luxuriance, heath and harvest. The poet's conclusions are polemically asserted in many of the shorter fragments; and two pieces in his comic-satiric manner arraign Nobodaddy, the non-existent father-god, for his endorsement of a prohibitive sexual code and a upas-like system of political oppression.

The lyrics associated with the bard were almost certainly written early in this phase of Blake's development, and their manner is less impassioned than that of 'A Song of Liberty' or Oothoon's last speech. The greatest of them, 'The Little Girl Lost' and 'The Little Girl Found', employ incantatory five-syllable lines to present a two-part story with a fairy-tale atmosphere; and their account of the virgin's reception among the wild animals is far removed from the polemical intensities of *The Marriage of Heaven and Hell*. Analogues to the substance of this narrative have been found in folklore, in *The Faerie Queene*, and in Milton's *Comus*; and it has been compared in particular with the Persephone myth, and with Neoplatonic interpretations of that myth which were available to Blake in the writings of Thomas Taylor. Lyca's resemblance to Persephone is indeed close, not only in her descent into a lower world but also in the parental expedition to rescue her; and Blake's deviations from the archetypal plot invite attention to spiritual allegory by largely eliminating hints of seasonal myth. There can be no doubt that these poems are in part concerned with the soul's descent into material existence and with the commitment of divine love to the soul's redemption; and comparison with the stories of Thel and Oothoon shows among other things that the lyrics offer Blake's most coherent version of this motif.

The more expansive versions leave one in no doubt, however, that this myth of the soul's descent also represents the virgin's growing awareness of sexuality; and if one approaches the Lyca poems from the stories of Thel and Oothoon one recognises not only the importance of their erotic dimension but also the potentially disturbing features of the lower world they describe. The sexual theme is emphasised by the first illustration, where Lyca appears as a young woman embracing her lover; and a recognition of this strand leads one to perceive Lyca's parents as a human couple responding anxiously to their daughter's adolescence. On the other hand, the uneasiness that we feel over Lyca's slumbers in the lion-king's palace refers us back to the bardic preludium, which was divided from the narrative by an emblematic serpent. From the bard's perspective, Lyca's descent appears as a separation of man from God, a reduction of the garden to a desert, a transformation of eternal humanity into sleeping earth; and although his dream of a universal regeneration has an air of prophetic authority, its effect is to postpone to the indefinite future that apocalyptic vision which Innocence affirmed as an everpresent reality.

Prophecy: 'The Tyger' and 'The Fly'

On 10 October 1793 Blake issued from his home in Lambeth a prospectus (Keynes 1966, 207–8) which announced that ten works were 'published and on Sale'. The most expensive were a large engraving of Job, which was to 'commence a Series of subjects from the Bible', and a large engraving of Edward and Elinor, which was to 'commence a Series of subjects' from English history. The cheapest were two visionary successors to the tractates, in which Blake sought through complementary emblem-sequences to reveal the analogous cyclical forms of national and individual experience. His plan for *The History of England* is known only from a list of subjects in the notebook (Keynes 1966, 208–9); but *The Gates of Paradise* was completed at this date as a book 'for children' (Keynes 1966, 209) and later refashioned as a book 'for the sexes' (Keynes 1966, 760–71). The other six items were described as 'illuminated Books . . . printed in Colours'; and with reference to these Blake claimed to have 'invented a method of Printing both Letter-press and Engraving in a style more ornamental, uniform, and grand, than any before discovered'. The illuminated books advertised included *The Book of Thel*, *The Marriage of Heaven and Hell* and *Visions of the Daughters of Albion*; and they also included 'Songs of Innocence . . . Octavo, with 25 designs, price 5s' and 'Songs of Experience . . . Octavo, with 25 designs, price 5s'. These last entries may well be statements of intention rather than fact, since the title page of *Songs of Experience* is dated 1794 and no extant copy of *Songs of Innocence and Experience* has exactly twenty-five plates in each part; but the engraving of the eighteen notebook poems was doubtless initiated before the end of 1793.

The other work listed in the 1793 prospectus was 'America, a

Prophecy, in Illuminated Printing. Folio, with 18 designs; price 10s 6d'. Having identified the Poetic Genius with 'the Spirit of Prophecy' in *All Religions Are One*, Blake developed his conception of prophetic utterance in *The Marriage of Heaven and Hell* through an imagined conversation with Isaiah and Ezekiel; and in the bardic lyrics he attributed prophetic visions and purposes to a poet-figure drawn from pre-Romantic medievalism. Like many authors of the late eighteenth century, Blake was disposed to seek literary models outside the Graeco-Roman tradition; and his growing desire to combine visionary idealism with denunciation of existing power-structures made it natural that he should emulate the manner and method of Old Testament prophecy. *America*, which was probably written late in 1792, was engraved with the date 1793 on its title page; and it was followed by another 'illuminated book' entitled *Europe: A Prophecy*, whose title page is dated 1794. Closely related to these self-styled prophecies is the shorter 'illuminated book' entitled *The Song of Los*, which is attributed to 'the Eternal Prophet' and divided into two sections headed *Africa* and *Asia*. The title page of *The Song of Los* is dated 1795, and like those of *Europe* and *America* it identifies the place of publication as Lambeth. Work in the prophetic mode was an important strand in Blake's literary activity around 1793–5, when the new plates for *Songs of Innocence and Experience* were being engraved.

In offering a mythical history of the American Revolution, *America* (Keynes 1966, 195–206; Erdman 1975, 137–55) communicates a London radical view of the forces at work in the French Revolution. The poem comprises a short preludium, which defines rebellion against confinement as an archetypal event, and a longer narrative, which presents the Anglo-American conflict as a historic instance of that archetype. The preludium shows a confrontation between a chained embodiment of fiery energy named Orc and a 'shadowy female' representing the material world which has confined and nourished him. At first she remains silent and elusive while he voices his demonic rage; but when his gathered frustration has broken his chains, she receives his fertilising power with a cry of ironic triumph. In the succeeding narrative the historic birth of rebellion is perceived by American and British leaders as a 'Human fire' over the Atlantic; and the implicit conflict of ideologies is dramatised in a debate between Orc, who proclaims the imminence of a revolutionary apocalypse, and Albion's Angel, who calls on the angels of his thirteen colonies to suppress the 'Eternal Viper'. Attempting to fight Orc's flames with plagues, Albion's Angel finds that these recoil on himself; and although the 'Demon red' is temporarily hidden by Urizen's snows, the poem declares the 'five gates' of oppression's 'law-built heaven' to have been destroyed. *America* is at once a vehement affirmation of Blake's apocalyptic revolutionism and a dramatically convincing evocation of the contrary states revealed in different visionary and rhetorical modes.

The conventions of prophetic writing legitimise not only magniloquence and dramatic confrontation but also obscurity and rhapsodic irregularity. Besides encompassing a larger subject than *America* and employing a greater diversity of mythical inventions, *Europe* (Keynes 1966, 237–45; Erdman 1975, 155–73) is largely composed in unrhymed lines of varying length; and it manifests in an acute form the discontinuity encouraged by Blake's idiosyncratic method of production. The poem's imaginative coherence is assured, however, by the complementary relationship between its preludium, in which the 'shadowy female' laments that 'mother Enitharmon' shapes every rebirth of energy into a new restrictive code, and its narrative, which traces the conflict between the eternal prophet Los and his counterpart Enitharmon through the historic cycle from the Christian nativity to the French Revolution. The preludium envisages the first matter as an inverted mystery-tree whose roots draw life out of eternity for its branches to consign into material existence. The first half of the narrative considers the birth of Christ as an example of this process, attributing the corruption of his redemptive power to Enitharmon's malice in declaring sexual love to be sinful. The second half of the narrative relates the climactic tyranny of modern Europe to a primeval descent into druidical religion, and associates Orc's reappearance 'in the vineyards of red France' with the release of Los's accumulated longing in an apocalyptic 'strife of blood'. In its vast scope, its prophetic extravagance and its bewildering variety of symbolic language, *Europe* is Blake's most astonishing poem to date.

The rhapsodic obscurity typical of the prophetic mode reaches its climax in *The Song of Los* (Keynes 1966, 245–8; Erdman 1975, 174–81), which is among other things a Blakean reinterpretation of Gray's 'The Bard'. As Edward I was dismayed in his moment of triumph to hear the last bard foretell the sorrows of his descendants and the glories of the Tudors, so Urizen turns pale at the time of the Fall when Los predicts the downward spiral of postlapsarian existence and the initiation of a Last Judgement by the Orc of the French Revolution. Condensed and cryptic as it is, this comprehensive vision of human history incorporates not only an attack on materialist philosophy but also a choric speech in which the kings of Asia recommend the economic policies of the Pitt regime. The prophetic manner is one in which extravagance and harsh topicality are readily united.

There are thematic analogies between these historico-mythical works on the four continents and the eighteen notebook poems incorporated in *Songs of Experience*; and the generic distinctions between prophecy and lyric not only conceal these analogies but also enhance their interest. The 'warlike men' of *America* are threatened with the 'heavy chain' that binds the speaker of 'Earth's Answer'; and the 'stored snows' that hide the flames of Orc are from the same 'icy magazines' as those endured by the chimney sweeper. The shadowy female's inverted mystery-tree reappears in the design for 'Holy Thursday', with a crucified boy among the oak-leaves of its downward branches; and the swaddling-clothes that 'compass' the rebellious child achieve cosmic significance in *Europe* and domestic reality in 'Infant Sorrow'. The 'nets and gins and traps' of *The Song of Los* are the 'mind-forg'd manacles' of 'London'; and the revolutionary apocalypse of the Eternal Prophet's vision is foreseen by the little vagabond as a merging of church and alehouse. The accents of Enitharmon and Urizen are audible in 'Nurse's Song' and 'A Poison Tree'; and many lyrics are devoted, like many speeches in the prophecies, to the precise articulation of imperfect understanding.

Blake's dramatic rendering of postlapsarian mental process is at its subtlest in the two poems, 'The Tyger' and 'The Fly', which together complement the innocent monologue of 'The Lamb'. Whereas the response of Innocence to another life was unaffected by distinctions in power, Experience reacts in quite different ways to beings more and less powerful than itself. As the speaker of 'The Tyger' interrogates the ambiguous image of beauty and terror which his incantatory questions are calling up, he perceives its fiery nature as a challenge to the ramifications of error, and is overawed by the strength and

vision of its hypothetical creator. Postulating for the tiger
a mysterious origin in the depths of matter or space, he
attributes its creation to a superhuman power combining the
audacity of Prometheus with the craftsmanship of Vulcan; and
as he struggles to envisage the divine artisan's technology he is
prompted to wonder and anguish by his growing apprehension
of creator and creature as one. Though he cannot sustain the
perception implicit in his unfinished questions, his subsequent
images of iron-working express a sharp and appreciative insight;
and though his understanding is still confused by the creator-
hypothesis, his new confidence is rewarded with a revelation of
heaven's regenerative surrender, which he sees as a fading of the
stars in the dawn. Through his final reiteration of the question
with which he began, he shows that his imaginative ordeal has
moved the balance of his uncertainty from fear to admiration.
The many influences which contributed to the visionary and
linguistic intensity of this lyric include a painting by Stubbs,
the views of eighteenth-century aestheticians on the sublime, the
fire-imagery used by Old Testament prophets writing about God's
anger, the attacks of anti-Jacobin propagandists on the 'tygerish
multitude', and a sequence of rhetorical questions about creation
in *The Divine Pymander of Hermes Trismegistus*. The poetic authority
which all critics have recognised emerges from a fusion of seemingly incompatible perceptions, in which a political manifesto
unites with a metaphysical investigation and a psychologically
intricate monologue is also a vividly particularised evocation of
Felis tigris.

'The Fly', which like 'The Tyger' has been the subject
of extensive critical debate, exposes the lethargic reasoning
with which a fallen mind explains its cruelty towards weaker
lives. Having injured or killed an insect, the speaker dissolves
his regret in sentimental philosophy. Oppressed by a sense of
helplessness, he finds a justification for his concern in the
notion that he is himself as defenceless as the fly; and though
he also propounds the potentially regenerative thesis that the
fly's life could be as precious as a man's, he fails to pursue
the implications of this insight. Assuming the fly's activity to
be idle and its suffering to have been idly caused, he dolefully
reduces man to the same level. Drifting into abstract theorising,
he finds a basis for his pessimism in the dogma that being consists
simply in cogitation; and this premise, which casually ignores

the modes of 'thought' acknowledged in line 3, is plausible enough to satisfy his unimpassioned intellect. His conclusion identifies human beings with insects and therefore dismisses the difference between life and death as unimportant; but the reader, perceiving an ambiguity in the word 'happy' that could reverse this destructive reasoning, apprehends the Blakean message that the smallest creature may be a world of delight, and formulates a correspondingly positive valuation of mankind. The illustration reinterprets this monologue as that of a woman who has bruised the sensibility of a child but is too beclouded by Experience to advance from regret into love; and by introducing the additional figure of a girl hitting a shuttlecock Blake completes his image of an emblematic cycle in which Innocence destroyed becomes a destroyer of Innocence.

Scripture: 'The Human Abstract'

Blake's imitation of the prophets in his visions of the American and French Revolutions was a special instance of that reinterpretation of scripture which occupied him from adolescence to old age. The prose-poem entitled 'Samson', which appeared in *Poetical Sketches*, was clearly designed as the start of a biblical epic like Gessner's *The Death of Abel*. His Swedenborgian period fostered his interest in those books which the New Church acknowledged as 'the Word'; and it also encouraged him to look for 'internal' or allegorical meanings in apparently prosaic texts. When he turned against Swedenborg in *The Marriage of Heaven and Hell*, the weapons he used included allusions to Job, Isaiah, Ezekiel and the gospels; and he not only professed to read the Bible in its 'infernal or diabolical sense' but also claimed to have a 'Bible of Hell' ready for publication. Like other writers of the nineties, he found Old Testament prophecy an appropriate vehicle for comment on contemporary affairs; and in the visionary extravagance and obscurity of his continental cycle he approached the vehemence of St John's attacks on Roman imperialism in Revelation.

The prophetic impulse, which drives the poet towards rhetorical excess and achieves its climactic subject in a Last Judgement, directs one of the main advances in Blake's non-lyrical writing of 1793–5. The other is controlled by an opposite impulse, which through intensity and concentration pursues not ultimate but primal truths, and discovers its essential subject in the Fall. The three works in which Blake seeks a deeper understanding of the Fall have title pages naming Lambeth as their place of publication; and the connection with his Bible of Hell is emphasised by a mechanical division of the text into numbered chapters and verses. Instead of the expansive and often irregular metres of the prophecies, these books are composed in hammered lines of three or four stresses; and their parodic refashioning of the biblical story has a stark physicality that makes it appear an exposure of bitter truths. The major characters, here as in the prophecies, are the sky-god Urizen and the eternal prophet Los; and Blake seems to associate them with the Elohim and Jehovah of the Hebrew Pentateuch, opposite powers who both appear in the Authorised Version as 'God'. As Los in the fallen state is taunted by his counterpart Enitharmon, so Urizen after rejecting eternity denounces his empress Ahania; and the rebellious Orc, now identified as the child of Los, finds an echo in Urizen's son Fuzon, whose revolt against his father is a display of Urizenic ambition. The poems' subject is the collective or individual breakdown which precipitates man into the conflict of fallen existence; and they explore that subject by restating the events of Genesis and Exodus in terms of these mythical beings who, like the classical deities, are both aspects of the mind and forces in the world.

The most ambitious of these three works is *The Book of Urizen* (Keynes 1966, 222–37; Erdman 1975, 182–210), which was initially called *The First Book of Urizen* but was renamed when Blake wrote the fifth chapter of its sequel. This poem, whose title page is dated 1794, consists of a short preludium and nine pseudo-biblical chapters, and offers a reinterpretation of Genesis 1–3. The first three chapters describe Urizen's withdrawal from eternity into solitary ratiocination, his proclamation of an authoritarian moral code, and his resultant collapse into material existence. The middle chapters show the shaping of Urizen's body by the blacksmith Los, the forming of Los's pity into a separate being named Enitharmon, and the discordant union of Los and Enitharmon which leads to the birth of Orc. The last three chapters record the binding of Orc with the Chain of Jealousy, Urizen's investigation of his fallen universe, and the commitment of humanity to an oppressed and restricted life in Africa. *The Book of Ahania* (Keynes 1966, 249–55; Erdman 1975, 211–13), which is in five chapters and dated 1795, offers a reinterpretation of Moses' departure from Egypt and of his acceptance of the commandments. The javelin of fire that Fuzon hurls against Urizen is answered by a poisoned rock, which is subsequently identified as Mount Sinai; and Fuzon's corpse, being nailed by Urizen to the Tree of Mystery, becomes in Asia the authority for an oppression worse than Pharaoh's. The book's title is finally justified by the eloquent monologue of Chapter 5, in which the weeping mother remembers the harmony that the exodus has destroyed. *The Book of Los* (Keynes 1966, 255–60; Erdman 1975, 214–15), whose title page is dated 1795, consists of a short preludium and a longer narrative; but this form is concealed, in ironic imitation of the Bible, by an arbitrary division into four chapters. In the lyrical preludium an aged prophetess recalls the prelapsarian state as one in which no impulse was deemed sinful and all desires were satisfied. The narrative, which complements the middle chapters of *The Book of Urizen*, is concerned with the Fall of Los and his prolonged struggle to re-attain human shape. Blake's rewriting of the Pentateuch explores the interrelationship of religious, political and familial authority; and its events have many parallels in myth, literature and history. The account of Fuzon's rebellion and defeat, for example, interprets the story of Moses in a way which implies analogous judgements on the life of Christ and on the progress of the French Revolution.

The Bible was to Blake the most important of all texts, but its significance did not differ in kind from that of other manifestations of the Poetic Genius. In the series of twelve large colour prints on which Blake began to work about 1795 (Butlin 1981, Catalogue 289–329 and Plates 384–419), biblical events are combined with Shakespearean and Miltonic motifs in the service of a Blakean vision; and an understanding of the sequence can be achieved only through imaginative response to its component parts. In *Elohim Creating Adam* a Urizenic creator imposes his will on a worm-entwined man; and in *Satan Exulting over Eve* a bat-winged militarist triumphs sadly over a serpent-bound woman. *God Judging Adam* shows a white-haired man bowing to a sun-god made in his own image; and *The Good and Evil Angels* shows how the products of demonic energy are received and moulded by the sun-god's agents. *Lamech and His Two Wives* shows the moment in Genesis 4: 9–24 when Lamech tells his wives that the man he has slain will be avenged 'seventy and sevenfold'; and *Naomi Entreating Ruth and Orpah* shows the moment in Ruth 1: 6–18 when Ruth announces that she will accompany Naomi to Bethlehem. *Nebuchadnezzar* illustrates the passage in Daniel 4: 28–37 where the Babylonian king eats grass and develops 'nails like birds' claws'; and *Newton* offers a similar design, in which the arch-materialist is using claw-like dividers to produce a mathematical diagram. *Hecate* shows the 'triple Hecate' of *A Midsummer Night's Dream* as moon-goddess and ruler of 'Vegetative Existence'; and *Pity* illustrates the lines in *Macbeth* about 'pity, like a naked new-born babe/Striding the blast'. Illustrating Adam's vision of the 'lazar-house' which is fallen life, *The House of Death* represents Milton's 'triumphant Death' as a blind sky-god dispensing pestilence from a legal scroll; and *Christ Appearing to the Apostles* illustrates the passage in Luke 24: 36–48 where the risen Christ preaches 'remission of sins' and helps his disciples to 'understand the scriptures'. These prints are among Blake's greatest artistic achievements, and their meaning as a sequence deserves more attention than it has yet received.

That *Songs of Innocence* affirms the ideal represented in Genesis by the Garden of Eden is evident from such poems as 'The Ecchoing Green'; but 'Spring' shows that the Edenic vision is apocalyptic also, and the reference to 'life's river' in 'Night' recalls Revelation 22: 1. The prophesied transformation of desert into garden in 'The Little Girl Lost' recalls Isaiah 35: 1, and the lines about the 'Holy Word' in the 'Introduction' to *Songs of Experience* allude to Genesis 3: 8. 'The Sick Rose' anticipates the first two colour prints in linking the Fall of Adam and Eve with an 'invisible worm' who is both Elohim and Satan; and that deity is connected with the speaker of 'A Poison Tree' through the Machiavel who plants 'a garden of fruits' in *The Book of Urizen* 7: 8. The inscription above the chapel door in 'The Garden of Love' recalls Deuteronomy 6: 9; and the 'Mystery' worshipped by the priest in 'A Little Boy Lost' is clearly the mother-harlot of Revelation 17: 5. 'The Clod and the Pebble' draws its second speaker from 1 Samuel 17: 40, where David chooses 'five smooth stones out of the brook' for his fight with Goliath; and the point of this allusion is clarified in the designs by the contrast between the frogs and the cattle.

The most powerful Fall-narrative in *Songs of Experience* is 'The Human Abstract', which displaced 'A Divine Image'

(Keynes 1966, 221; Erdman 1975, 389) as counterpart for 'The Divine Image' of *Songs of Innocence*. Though it originated as a devil's song (Keynes 1966, 164), 'The Human Abstract' is a grimly concentrated psychological allegory which purports to show how the vocabulary of Innocence can become the seedplot of sacrificial religion. Man's withdrawal from the enactment to the contemplation of impulse having formulated the concepts of pity and mercy, an independent value comes to be placed on these; and the speaker contends that such idolatry stealthily propagates the suffering on which its idols thrive. The resultant distrust having established the ominous peace of an arms-race, the desires repressed in that peace become the forms of self-love from which Urizenic reasoning expects public benefits; and moralistic calculation now plans the exploitation of life like a professional birdcatcher. Having withdrawn into mock-Innocence so that his devices can operate, he evolves the technique of 'seeming diffidence' to explain the gulf between his inaction and his pretence of concern; and the presenting of self-interest as self-denial becomes an obscurantism which darkens man's understanding and houses a parasitic priesthood. When this mystery-tree is fully developed, unfallen beings are tempted to emulate their oppressors' dishonesty; and the ravenous selfhood waits to devour the sacrificed longings of those who yield. The mythical narrative of stanza 6 declares this upas-like process to be a disease of the mind; but that declaration, as the last line shows, expresses not dismissive optimism but grim recognition. The critique of Genesis implicit in this lyric is clarified by the narrative of *The Book of Urizen*; and Blake's picture of the birdcatcher entangled in his own net is further explained by Chapter 3 of *The Book of Ahania*.

Redemption: 'To Tirzah'

All but one of the poems finally included in *Songs of Innocence and Experience* had been engraved by the end of 1795, and the book gave every appearance of being complete. It reflected, more comprehensively than any other engraved book of 1788–95, the range of Blake's interests over those eight years; and as a two-part sequence of dramatic lyrics it also fulfilled the promise of its title page by 'shewing the Two Contrary States of the Human Soul'. The variety of its artistic techniques was harmonised by a consistent approach to colouring in each copy; and a particular interpretation of its diverse perspectives was suggested by the selection of 'The Clod and the Pebble' as the final plate. Having brought *Songs of Innocence and Experience* to this degree of perfection, Blake turned from the production of engraved books to ambitious projects in other visual and literary modes.

A major activity of the London booksellers at this time was the production of standard works in large illustrated editions; and about 1795 Blake undertook to design illustrations for Edward Young's religio-philosophical poem *Night Thoughts*. Young's poem is divided into nine nights, the last and longest of which is concerned with the Last Judgement; and each of Blake's designs was initially produced as a watercolour surrounding a page of printed text. The first volume of the projected edition was published in 1797, with the designs engraved by Blake himself; but critical reactions were mixed, and low sales discouraged the booksellers from proceeding. The watercolours show Blake transposing Young's abstract reasoning into visionary statement: the dead metaphors of the text are disconcertingly resurrected, and many designs are not illustrations but rather satiric inversions of Young's moralistic argument. Despite the commercial failure of his undertaking, Blake went on to produce comparable illustrations for other works: a series for the poems of Gray, again as watercolours surrounding the text; full-page designs for Blair's *The Grave*, which were engraved by Luigi Schiavonetti and published in 1808; sequences of full-page watercolours illustrating and reinterpreting six poems by Milton; a book of engravings which converted the story of Job into a closely-wrought argument about the letter and the spirit; and a sequence of watercolours which offered a critical commentary on the *Divina Commedia* of Dante. These series of designs are the major artistic works of Blake's later career; and they expound, through intricately-related celebration and criticism of the texts illustrated, a Christianity whose leading principles are the primacy of the imagination and the forgiveness of sin.

The *Night Thoughts* project affected the format of Blake's other great undertaking of the late nineties, the long narrative-poem in seven-stress lines which was known initially as *Vala* and finally as *The Four Zoas* (Keynes 1966, 263–382). In this expansive and ambitious work Blake sought to reorganise the events of the Lambeth books into a coherent mythical epic; and the surviving manuscript shows that his conception of that epic underwent large changes as his beliefs evolved over a period of years. Within the nine-night framework suggested by *Night Thoughts*, the poem traces man's imaginative history from the Fall to the Last Judgement through the interaction of four pairs of mythical characters: Los, who is imagination, and his counterpart Enitharmon; Urizen, who is reason, and his counterpart Ahania; Luvah, who is emotion, and his counterpart Vala; and Tharmas, who is instinct, and his counterpart Enion. As Blake's ideology develops, these characters become aspects of the 'Eternal Man' Albion and his counterpart Jerusalem; and Blake's renewed insistence on imagination and forgiveness leads him to associate Albion's 'fall into division' with the death of Lazarus and to emphasise the role of the Lamb of God in bringing about his 'resurrection to unity'. Although *The Four Zoas* was never engraved, much of its mythical and scriptural argument found its way into the two large engraved books of Blake's later career, the book of fifty plates which he called *Milton* (Keynes 1966, 480–535; Erdman 1975, 216–67) and the book of one hundred plates which he called *Jerusalem* (Keynes 1966, 620–747; Erdman 1975, 280–379).

Having acquired some knowledge of New Testament Greek, Blake took a text from Ephesians as epigraph for *The Four Zoas*; and late additions to that poem make extensive use of the passage in John 11: 1–46 about Christ's raising of Lazarus, the brother of Martha and Mary. Another biblical motif that gathers new significance in Blake's later work is the crucifixion, which figures prominently in the late additions to *The Four Zoas* and in *Jerusalem*. Crucifixion as the tormenting of a sacrificial victim is connected with the notion of druidical religion which Blake drew from eighteenth-century antiquarians; and the central roles among the torturers are taken by two figures of biblical origin whom he calls Rahab and Tirzah. In each of these Blake identifies two unrelated biblical uses of the same name. Rahab is the harlot who conceals the Israelite spies in Joshua 2: 1–22, and she is also the woman-serpent of Psalms 89: 10; Blake thus converts a traditional emblem of the church into a hostile image of institutional religion, which he then connects with the seven churches of Asia in Revelation 1: 11. Tirzah is the capital city of the northern kingdom, which is frequently mentioned in the historical books as rival and opponent of Jerusalem. Since Jerusalem is for Blake the heavenly city of Revelation 21: 9–27, Tirzah as antithesis to Jerusalem becomes an emblem of worldly dominion; but Jerusalem is also the separated counterpart of Albion, and the northern capital is therefore identified with the Tirzah who appears in Numbers 27: 1–11 as one of the five daughters of Zelophehad. For the unimaginative reader this passage is concerned with the law of inheritance; but Blake, pursuing the 'internal sense', connects the daughters of Zelophehad with that 'philosophy of the five senses' which has been perfected by Bacon, Newton and Locke. The name Tirzah is thus linked both with worldly authority and with materialistic thought; and the five senses complement the seven churches to make up the twelve sadistic Daughters of Albion, who are associated in turn with the twelve stones of Joshua 4: 1–9 and of Exodus 28: 15–21.

The speaker of 'To Tirzah' affirms that all life in the fallen world must commit itself to the fires of a Last Judgement in order to rise above the twofold vision of mortality; and he rejects the parental claims of the nature-goddess in the words uttered by Christ to his mother in John 2: 4. This clarity of vision allows him to interpret the Fall as a dividing of humanity by the twin errors of self-abasement and self-aggrandisement; and he perceives that man has been saved from a descent into non-entity by the creation of time, which affords the possibility of regaining eternity through creative endeavour. He rejects as hypocritical the nature-goddess' expectation that he should acquiesce in the binding of perception within the fallen senses; and through his faith in the redemptive power of incarnate divinity he rises above his sense of dependence on the material universe. The enigmatic illustration shows a dying man being held by two women beneath a tree with seven apples, while a white-bearded man prepares to anoint him from a sacred vessel. This ambiguous image invites us to see that the Urizenic literalism with which Rahab and Tirzah inhibit Albion's resurrection is a parodic inversion of the regenerative faith shown by the sisters of Lazarus. Inscribed vertically on the old man's robes are the words 'It is Raised a Spiritual Body'; and this text refers us to the eloquent passage in 1 Corinthians 15: 39–45 where St Paul expounds the antithesis on which this plate is founded.

After the engraving of 'To Tirzah', Blake made no further addition to the text of *Songs of Innocence and Experience*; but he continued to produce new copies, in which alterations of colouring and plate-sequence expressed his gradually-changing attitude to the 'Contrary States'. The use of 'The Clod and the Pebble' as endpiece to copies C and D suggests that Blake was still disposed around 1795 to see Experience as a corrective to Innocence; but copy E, in which he introduces 'To Tirzah' as endpiece and omits 'The Clod and the Pebble' entirely, indicates that his view of the book has undergone a radical change. Only in his last years, when the composition of these songs was far behind him, did he achieve that unpolemical appreciation of both Innocence and Experience which is expressed in the regular plate-sequence of the late copies. In those copies the keynote of Innocence is sounded in pastoral songs like 'The Shepherd' and 'The Lamb', and its summation is the proclamation of total responsiveness in 'On Another's Sorrow'. 'The Clod and the Pebble' is introduced at the first opportunity as a typical expression of the worldview of Experience; and 'To Tirzah' is located unemphatically two plates from the end. The penultimate poem is 'The School-Boy', whose discontent appears mild after the intensities of 'London' and 'The Human Abstract'; and the endpiece is 'The Voice of the Ancient Bard', whose summons to a new life can be viewed as an epilogue to *Songs of Innocence and Experience* as a whole.

In imaginative terms, the new developments initiated by the illustrations to Young were sustained to the end of Blake's life; but in worldly terms they ended with the commercial failure of the *Night Thoughts* project in 1797. In 1800 Blake moved from Lambeth to a cottage at Felpham on the Sussex coast, where he enjoyed the patronage of William Hayley and was employed on the engravings for Hayley's *Life of Cowper*. Tensions arose because Hayley's concern for Blake's material welfare conflicted with Blake's commitment to 'the Divine Vision'; and in 1803 Blake returned to London and settled at 17 South Molton Street. His hopes of worldly prosperity were disappointed in 1805, when the commission for engraving his Blair designs was given to Schiavonetti, and again in 1809, when an exhibition of his paintings at his brother's house attracted little interest. His poverty was alleviated by Thomas Butts, a civil servant who regularly bought his work; and after 1818 he attracted a group of younger artists, who admired his paintings and believed in his visions. In 1821 he moved into two first-floor rooms at 3 Fountain Court between the Strand and the Thames; and he died there in 1827, with the Dante illustrations still unfinished. His wife, to whose lifelong devotion many reports bear witness, survived until 1831.

References

This is a list of the scholarly and critical works mentioned in the text. The books marked with three asterisks are essential for any serious study. Those marked with two asterisks are of varying quality, but all contain extensive discussion of *Songs of Innocence and Experience*. The books marked with one asterisk are major studies of Blake's literary work as a whole.

Adlard, John, *The Sports of Cruelty*, London: Cecil and Amelia Woolf, 1972.

Acrs, David, Jonathan Cook and David Punter, *Romanticism and Ideology: Studies in English Writing 1765–1830*, London, Boston and Henley: Routledge and Kegan Paul, 1981.

Beer, John, *Blake's Humanism*, Manchester: Manchester University Press; New York: Barnes and Noble, 1968.

Bentley, G.E. (ed.), *William Blake's Writings*, 2 vols, Oxford: Oxford University Press, 1978.

Berger, P., *William Blake: Poet and Mystic*, 1914; reprint, New York: Hansell House PUblishers, 1968.

Bindman, David, *Blake as an Artist*, Oxford: Phaidon, 1977.

*Bloom, Harold, *Blake's Apocalypse: A Study in Poetic Argument*, London: Victor Gollancz, 1963.

Blunt, Anthony, *The Art of William Blake*, London: Oxford University Press, 1959.

**Bottrall, Margaret (ed.), *William Blake, Songs of Innocence and Experience: A Casebook*, London and Basingstoke: Macmillan, 1970.

Bronowski, J., *William Blake and the Age of Revolution*, London: Routledge and Kegan Paul, 1972.

Butlin, Martin, *The Paintings and Drawings of William Blake*, 2 vols, New Haven and London: Yale University Press, 1981.

Crehan, Stewart, *Blake in Context*, Dublin: Gill and Macmillan, 1984.

*Damon, S. Foster, *William Blake: His Philosophy and Symbols*, London, Bombay and Sydney: Constable, 1924.

Dike, Donald, 'The Difficult Innocence: Blake's Songs and Pastoral', *English Literary History*, XXVIII (1961) 353–75.

Dyson, A.E., ' "The Little Black Boy": Blake's Song of Innocence', *Critical Quarterly*, I (1959), 44–7.

*Erdman, David V., *Blake, Prophet against Empire: A Poet's Interpretation of the History of His Own Times*, Princeton: Princeton University Press, 1954.

Erdman, David V. (ed.), *The Poetry and Prose of William Blake*, New York: Doubleday and Company, 1965.

Erdman, David V. (ed.), *The Notebook of William Blake*, London: Oxford University Press, 1973.

Erdman, David V. (ed.), *The Illuminated Blake*, London: Oxford University Press, 1975.

Erdman, David V., and John E. Grant (eds), *Blake's Visionary Forms Dramatic*, Princeton: Princeton University Press, 1970.

Essick, Robert N., *William Blake: Printmaker*, Princeton: Princeton University Press, 1980.

Fauvet, Paul, 'Mind-forg'd manacles – Blake and Ideology', *Red Letters*, no. 6 (n.d.), 16–39.

*Frye, Northrop, *Fearful Symmetry: A Study of William Blake*, Princeton: Princeton University Press, 1947.

Frye, Northrop (ed.), *Blake: A Collection of Critical Essays*, Englewood Cliffs: Prentice-Hall, 1966.

Gallagher, Phillip J., 'The Word Made Flesh: Blake's "A Poison Tree" and the Book of Genesis', *Studies in Romanticism*, XVI (1977), 237–49.

Gardner, Stanley, *Blake*, London: Evans Brothers, 1968.

**Gardner, Stanley, *Blake's 'Innocence' and 'Experience' Retraced*, London: Athlone Press; New York: St Martin's Press, 1986.

**Gillham, D.G., *Blake's Contrary States: The 'Songs of Innocence and of Experience' as Dramatic Poems*, Cambridge: Cambridge University Press, 1966.

**Gleckner, Robert F., *The Piper and the Bard: A Study of William Blake*, Detroit: Wayne State University Press, 1959.

Glen, Heather, 'The Poet in Society: Blake and Wordsworth in London', *Literature and History*, No. 3 (March 1976), 2–28.

**Glen, Heather, *Vision and Disenchantment: Blake's 'Songs' and Wordsworth's 'Lyrical Ballads'*, Cambridge: Cambridge University Press, 1983.

Hagstrum, Jean H., 'William Blake's "The Clod and the Pebble" ', *Restoration and Eighteenth Century Literature: Essays in Honor of Alan Dugald McKillop*, Edited by Carroll Camden, Chicago: University of Chicago Press, 1963, 381–8.

Hagstrum, Jean H., *William Blake, Poet and Painter: An Introduction to the Illuminated Verse*, Chicago: University of Chicago Press, 1964.

Harper, George M., 'The Source of Blake's "Ah! Sunflower" '. *Modern Language Review*, XLVIII (1953), 139–42.

**Hirsch E.D., *Innocence and Experience: An Introduction to Blake*, New Haven and London: Yale University Press, 1964.

**Holloway, John, *Blake: The Lyric Poetry*, London: Edward Arnold, 1968.

***Keynes, Geoffrey (ed.), *The Complete Writings of William Blake*, London: Oxford University Press, 1966.

***Keynes, Geoffrey (ed.), *Songs of Innocence and Of Experience: Shewing the Two Contrary States of the Human Soul*, London: Oxford University Press, 1970.

King Hele, Desmond, *Erasmus Darwin and the Romantic Poets*, Basingstoke and London: Macmillan, 1986.

**Larrissy, Edward, *William Blake*, Oxford and New York: Basil Blackwell, 1985.

**Leader, Zachary, *Reading Blake's 'Songs'*, Boston, London and Henley: Routledge and Kegan Paul, 1981.

Leavis, F.R., *Revaluation: Tradition and Development in English Poetry*, London: Chatto and Windus, 1936.

Lister, Raymond, *William Blake: An Introduction to the Man and to His Work*, London: G. Bell and Sons, 1968.

Manlove, C.N., 'Engineered Innocence: Blake's "The Little Black Boy" and "The Fly" ', *Essays in Criticism*, XXVII (1977), 112–21.

Margoliouth, H.M., *William Blake*, London: Oxford University Press, 1951.

Mitchell, W.J.T., *Blake's Composite Art: A Study of the Illuminated Poetry*, Princeton: Princeton University Press, 1978.

Nurmi, Martin K., *William Blake*, London: Hutchinson, 1975.

Paley, Morton D., *Energy and the Imagination: A Study of the Development of Blake's Thought*, London: Oxford University Press, 1970.

Phillips, Michael (ed.), *Interpreting Blake*, Cambridge: Cambridge University Press, 1978.

Pinto, Vivian de Sola, 'Isaac Watts and William Blake', *Review of English Studies*, XX (1944), 214–23.

Pinto, Vivian de Sola (ed.), *The Divine Vision: Studies in the Poetry and Art of William Blake*, London: Victor Gollancz, 1957.

*Raine, Kathleen, *Blake and Tradition*, 2 vols, London: Routledge and Kegan Paul, 1969.

Raine, Kathleen, *William Blake*, London: Thames and Hudson, 1970.

Shrimpton, Nick, 'Hell's Hymn Book: Blake's *Songs of Innocence and of Experience* and Their Models', *Literature of the Romantic Period, 1750–1850*, Edited by R.T. Davies and B.G. Beatty, New York: Barnes and Noble, 1976, 19–35.

Stevenson, W.H. (ed.), *The Poems of William Blake*, London: Longman, 1971.

Swinburne, A.C., *William Blake: A Critical Essay*, 2nd ed., London: John Camden Hotten, 1868.

Todd, Ruthven, *William Blake: The Artist*, London: Studio Vista; New York: E.P. Dutton and Company, 1971.

**Wicksteed, Joseph H., *Blake's Innocence and Experience: A Study of the Songs and Manuscripts 'Shewing the Two Contrary States of the Human Soul'*, London and Toronto: J.M. Dent and Sons; New York: E.P. Dutton and Company, 1928.

Wilson, Mona, *The Life of William Blake*, 1927, rev. 1971; reprint St Albans: Granada Publishing, 1978.

Index to Poems

Index to Critics